Fabulous Rag Rugs from Simple Frames

OTHER TITLES BY THE AUTHOR

Rugmaker's Handbook Series:
#1 Knitted Rag Rugs for the Craftsman
#2 Fabulous Rag Rugs from Simple Frames

Other titles:
Traditional Shirred and Standing Wool Rugs
Crocheted and Fabric Tapestry Rugs
Bohemian Braid Rugs for the Beginner
Multi-strand Braids for Flat-Braided Rugs
Flat Wrap Rugs and Baskets
Introduction to Patched Rugs
Amish Knot Rugs
Broomstick Rugs
Chain Braid Rugs
Wagon Wheel Rugs
Anchored Loop Rugs (American Locker Hooking with Rags)
Bodkin Rugs
Introduction to Tambour Rugs
Knotted Shag Rugs
Pjonging and the Single Strand Chain Braids
"Hook Braided" Rugs; the Two-strand Attached Chain Braid
Kitchen Table Rugs
String Crochet Rugs
Primitive Rug Hooking, An Introduction
"Beaded" Rugs, A Unique Standing Wool Rug
A Rugmaker's Sampler

Rugmaker's Handbook No. 2

Fabulous Rag Rugs from Simple Frames

written and illustrated by,
Master Rugmaker
Diana Blake Gray

Rafter-four Designs
Cocolalla, Idaho

Rugmaker's Handbook No. 2
Fabulous Rag Rugs from Simple Frames

All Rights Reserved, Copyright 2004 by Diana Blake Gray

No part of this book may be reproduced or transmitted in any form or by any means, graphic, electronic, or mechanical, including photocopying, recording, taping, or by any information storage and/or retrieval system without the written permission of the publisher.

Rafter-four Designs

For information address:
Rafter-four Designs
P O Box 40
Cocolalla, ID 83813
http://www.rugmakershomestead.com

including information from:
A Rugmaker's Sampler, Copyright 1986 by Diana Blake Gray
Knotted Shag Rugs, Copyright 1999 by Diana Blake Gray
Kitchen Table Rugs, Copyright 1999 by Diana Blake Gray

SHORT EXCERPTS FROM THE TEXT MAY BE PUBLISHED WHEN INCORPORATED IN A REVIEW. HOWEVER, CRAFT WRITERS AND EDITORS SHOULD BE ADVISED THAT SEVERAL OF THE METHODS INCLUDED IN THIS BOOK ARE PUBLISHED HERE FOR THE FIRST TIME. DERIVATIVE ARTICLES AND WRITTEN WORKS MUST INCLUDE SPECIFIC CREDITS.

ISBN: 1-931426-27-9

Printed in the United States of America

Dedication

To my grandmother,
Grace Maria Converse Blake (1905-2001),
a magnificent teacher with the soul of an artist.
With love.

Contents

Preface .... *xiii*

How to Use This Book .... *xvii*

Introduction: *Frame Made Rag Rugs in Context* 1

PART I:
NON-TENSIONING METHODS
USING A PEGGED FRAME

Chapter 1: Making and Warping the Frame 2
    Preparing the warp
    Putting the warp on the frame
    Warping an old Frame

Chapter 2: Knotted Shag Rugs 7
    Knotted shag rug technique
    Knotting
    Removing from the frame
    Knots too loosely packed
    Making a rug without a nap
    Working with very light or slick fabrics
    Adding extra fringe to the sides of the rug
    Joining small sections to make a large rug
    High-Speed Knotted Shag Rugs
    A note to weavers using rug looms

Chapter 3: Those Darned Rugs.......... 20
 How to avoid "waisting"
 Basic Darned Rug Technique
 Worked one row at a time
 Worked back-and-forth
 Figure-8 Darned Rug
 Fine points of Darned Rugs
 Darning continuously back-and-forth in rows
 To change strip in middle of a row
 Removing the rug from the frame
 Finishing the rug
 Joining darned sections to make a large rug
 Making large darned rugs in a single section

Chapter 4: Amish Knot Rugs.......... 33
 FrameAmish knot technique
 Fine points of Amish knot rugs
 Working continuously back and forth with the Amish knot
 Removing the rug from frame
 Finishing the rug
 Insetting a design in an Amish knot rug
 Seed Corn Rugs

Chapter 5: Bess Chet Rugs.......... 40
 Basic Bess Chet technique
 The fine points of the Bess Chet rug
 Making a reversible rug
 Raised Bess Chet rugs
 Tambour Bess Chet Technique

Chapter 6: Twined Rugs 49
 Basic Twining
 Needlewoven (Shortcut Twining Worked Straight)

Chapter 7: Locker Hooking 56
 Locker hooking technique adapted for frames
 The fine points of locker hooking

Chapter 8: Advanced Techniques with Non-tensioning Methods 64
    Making large rugs in a single section
    Weaving warp strands back into the rug
    Combining non-tensioning techniques
    Inlays
    Free Standing Patterns, the Padula duck, the spider mum, the calico rainbow
    Freeform shaping of rugs
    Shaping three dimensional projects

Chapter 9: Non-tensioning Methods Worked Vertically 77
    Flat Wrap
    The fine points of the flat wrap
    Figure-Eight Wrap
    Two-Strand Figure-Eight Wrap

PART II:
NON-TENSIONING METHODS USING A BI-DIRECTIONAL WARP

Chapter 10: Modified Taaniko and Soumak 86
    Creating the frame and bi-directional warp
    Modified Soumak
    Working patterns into the rug
    Modified Taaniko
    Using multiple strands

Chapter 11: Rya Knotting on a Bi-directional warp 93

Chapter 12: Modified Hooked Rugs 98
    Hooking technique for frames
    Using the anchored loop technique for rugs

PART III: WEAVING TECHNIQUES FOR USE WITH FRAMES

Chapter 13: Weaving on a Pegged Frame 101
 Using a pegged frame as a "walking frame"
 Method for weaving longer projects
 What do I do with the side pegs?
 Using combinations of techniques to avoid tension problems

Chapter 14: Straight Weaving on a Flat Frame 109
 Constructing and preparing a flat frame for weaving
 Fabrics used for weaving on flat frames
 Straight weaving
 For a fringed end or side
 For a finished end or side
 For a bound edge
 Making a rug longer than your frame
 Diagonal weaving
 Simple twill and tabby patterns
 Using fabric and yarn together

Chapter 15: Frame Braids 118
 Frame wrapping
 Creating a frame braid
 For a finished end

Chapter 16: Wagon Wheel Rugs in Round and Oval Shapes 123
 Round rug technique
 Adding warp strands
 The fine points of wagon wheel rugs
 Making an oval wagon wheel rug

PART IV:
WEIRD AND WONDERFUL WARPS

Chapter 17: Twisted Warp Techniques 130
    Using a flat frame with twisted warps
    Using a Pegged Frame
    Using a Hanging Frame

Chapter 18: Spider Web Warp 140
    Creating square and rectangular warps

Chapter 19: The "Fifth Stick" Frame 145
    Easy tension control for tied warps

Chapter 20: Suspended Warps on Pegged Frames 149
    Creating a ¼-inch spacing with pegs on one-inch centers

Chapter 21: The Cheater's Warp
    Using fabric for a one-piece warp
    Attaching fabric to straight frames
    The fine points of the cheater's warp
    Making odd-shaped rugs
    Using the cheater's warp with light fabrics on a hanging frame

Chapter 22: Scroll Frame Warps 158
    One-way continuous warp
    Reversing a continuous warp

PART V:
HANDBOOK

Tools Needed in Addition to a Frame 163
   Lacing needles, locker hooks, cutting tools, basic sewing tools, folding tools

Tips for Handling Large Frames 165

Fabric Selection and Preparation 166
   Light woven cottons, single-knit fabrics, heavier and lighter knits, wool fabrics, novelty fabrics, denim, canvas and other heavy cotton fabrics

Estimating Fabric Consumption 170
Tearing vs. Cutting Fabrics 171

Joining Fabric Strips for Rug Making 172
   Overlapping bias joint, regular bias joint, no-sew ways to add strip or change colors, the bow tie joint

Spinning Warp or Weft Strips 175
Double-folding Warp and Weft strip 176
Triple-folding Strips for Flat Profile Rugs 179

Using Alternate Materials for Rugs 179
Lacing Rug Sections Together 181

Using a "Pinned" Frame 185
A Miscellany about Frames 187
Caring for Frame Rugs 189

Key to the Rugs on the Covers 191
Afterword 193
About the Author 195

Preface

I receive dozens of letters each year, which read something like this. "I really want to weave a rag rug but I can't afford (or don't have room for) a loom. Can I make one on a frame?" It is for those folks that this book is written. Not only can a wonderful rag rug be woven on a frame, but there are many types of fabulous rugs that can be made on a frame that just can't be made on a loom. I know that statement will seem like heresy to many dedicated weavers, but it is true.

It's not that I don't love weaving on a loom. In fact, weaving was the first formal textile training that I had when I was still a teenager. What I came to realize though is that a frame and a loom are two completely different tools and what works on one of them doesn't necessarily work on the other. So if you have ever suffered from "loom-envy," you can now approach rug making without apology, knowing that with a simple frame, you can make rugs that *can't* be made on a loom.

This is the first book to treat the frame as a distinct tool and explore the range of its potential. A frame is not just a pseudo-loom, nor should it be regarded as a substitute for a loom. It was the precursor of the loom, of course, and with the advances in weaving in the past centuries, the basic frame—and its uses—got lost along the way.

Most of the techniques here have never appeared in print but I won't claim to have invented them. Considering the vast pre-historic use of frames for textile construction, it is much more likely that I've simply rediscovered these methods. In developing the techniques in this book, I strove to apply the same logic in solving the same problems that faced ancient peoples all over the world. The result is a whole range of techniques, some so intuitive as to have been undoubtedly worked in ages past. Others are the result of the cross-pollination from other textile and rug making traditions.

Because the number of rug making methods appropriate for a frame is quite large—and there are limits to the size of the book—I didn't attempt to cover the so-called "off-loom weaving" methods that have already been heavily documented. Instead this book focuses on the frame methods that are new to modern fiber artists.

If you are interested in such off-loom techniques as back strap weaving or card weaving, there are many books available. If you are interested in weaving rugs on a loom, I can't recommend any books more highly than those of Peter Collingwood and, of course, for a full exploration of twined rugs, Bobbi Irwin's book "*Twined Rugs*" (Krause Publications, 2000) is the one you want.

On the other hand, if you are interested in exploring some new (ancient) techniques for making rugs, or you just want to put grandma's rug frame to use, this is just the book for you.

Acknowledgements

I want to thank everyone who has been so patient waiting for this book to reach completion. Your reminders and gentle nagging kept the project alive when so many others demanded attention. I hope the four years has been worth the wait.

I couldn't write a book about weaving in any form without thanks to Peter Strauss, who taught me to weave nearly forty years ago. His generosity in sharing the skills handed down through the hundreds of years of his family's weaving profession had a profound effect on this impressionable teenager. His dictum "Hand made should never look home-made" has guided my own work and been passed on to my students.

Finally, my thanks to Peter Collingwood in England for showing me that being a textile structuralist is at least a *respectable* form of insanity.

How to Use This Book

This isn't a "craft" book—instead it is a handbook for the textile explorer. You won't find instructions to make just one rug. Instead this book is a teaching tool and reference. You'll learn how to do each technique and then make it your own with color, design and variations. You'll probably find one or two of the rug methods are more attractive than the others and want to specialize and explore those methods yourself. Each technique has a world of possibilities.

Because this handbook includes so many diffferent methods, it has the potential to be overwhelming to a first-time rug maker. Nearly all of the techniques can be done by a beginner, and for those that are more complex, I've suggested another method to start with as a preliminary step to understanding the process.

This also isn't a book about weaving as such. You won't find the weaver's jargon used very often—although I do refer to the structural strands of the rugs as "warp." You do not need any particular textile experience to make these rugs.

There are five parts of the book. In each of the first four, rug making techniques are organized by the characteristics of the method (tensioning or non-tensioning), the type of frame, and the style of the warping. You do not need to begin in Part I and work progressively forward (although the easiest of the techniques are there). If you are more interested in making a Wagon Wheel rug for example, begin with Part II instead.

The parts of the book include:

- **Part I: Non-tensioning Methods Using a Pegged Frame.** Although these non-woven rugs can be made on any type of frame, pegged frames are used for the beginning rug maker, since the warp spacing is fixed by the pegs. These techniques use the pegs on only two sides of the frame, and many are simple enough for children to work.

- **Part II: Non-tensioning Methods Using a Bi-directional Warp.** These non-woven structures use pegs on all four sides of a frame.

- **Part III: Weaving Techniques for Use with Frames.** These are woven rugs, which are adapted to several types of frames, for those who do want to weave a rug—including round and oval rugs.

- **Part IV: Weird and Wonderful Warps.** The textile explorer will have a lot of fun with these techniques from spider web warps to the cheater's warp.

- **Part V. Handbook.** This is the general reference section with information that applies to all of the rugs. It is suggested that you look through the Handbook before you begin on any of the rugs, just to get an idea of the information that is available there.

The rugs in this book are an all-fabric construction making them very strong, thick and durable. However, they can also be adapted to other materials (yarn, cord, etc.) so if you don't have the time to devote to fabric preparation, you can still make most of these rugs. The Handbook section includes a discussion of appropriate substitutions of materials.

INTRODUCTION
Frame Made Rag Rugs in Context

Loom-woven rag rugs (also known as rag carpeting) have been a decorating staple for years and became a respected item of the country decorating style in the 19th and 20th centuries. Not so with the frame made rugs. Part of the difference is that too many of the rugs made on frames were simply an imitation of the loom weaving process (string warp, fabric weft) and since frames are not easily adapted to that style, the rugs were generally of a poorer quality.

Most rug frames were home made, though in the early part of the 19th century mail-order houses such as Sears, offered pre-built frames often with a full complement of pegs. Small frames for yarn weaving were sold through the 1960's and similar small frames for weaving hot pads with "sock loops" are still available in toy and craft stores. These small frames had the unfortunate side effect of convincing people that the larger pegged frames could also be used for weaving in the same way. Of course, that didn't work, and many of the antique wooden pegged frames have been idle for decades because they were just too large to accommodate the standard weaving procedure.

The biggest distinction between frames and looms is that most of the frame types are rigid while looms have mechanisms that allow for the adjustment of the tension of the warp threads. If you have ever tried to weave on a frame, even a very small one, you know that as each row of weft (cross threads) are woven through the warp, the warp gets tighter and tighter. At some point, weaving becomes impossible unless there is a way to release the tension on the warp.

In this book, you'll find that the techniques are divided up into "tensioning" and "non-tensioning" methods. The former will tighten the warp threads (like weaving) while the latter do not create stress on the warp. It is these non-tensioning techniques that are the most suitable for using on a frame. They are also the easiest to learn and come in a wide variety of textures.

An added bonus to the non-tensioning rug making methods is that the rugs themselves are thicker and softer than woven rugs, making them ideal for use where shock absorption is a consideration. Use them anywhere you do a lot of standing. Being made entirely of fabric, these rugs are also much more durable and less likely to bunch up or skid across the floor than the lighter weight rugs, so they can also be used at an entry or in heavy traffic areas.

PART I:
NON-TENSIONING METHODS USING A PEGGED FRAME

CHAPTER 1
Making and Warping the Frame

At this moment there aren't any commercially-made pegged frames for rug making, although I expect that to change soon. Luckily, the basic high-low pegged frame is quite easily built with simple materials. Of course, rug frames can be built in any size, but for your first frame, I really recommend keeping it small. The one square foot size is ideal for sampling a variety of the rug making methods and is easy to handle as you are learning. You can also assemble the squares into a larger rug, so even with the small frame you can create a large rug.

Another advantage of using a small frame is simply psychological. The square foot sections are quickly made and being able to see progress quickly is gratifying to beginning rug makers. Also, if you have a mobile lifestyle, the small frame can go with you more easily than a larger one.

If you already have a flat frame that you want to use, all you need to do is add the "pegs" which can be small nails, screws or wooden dowels. Craft stores sell fancy pegs already made, which will also work. The sample frame shown uses 1" X 2" finished lumber, which is available at home improvement stores. All four sides are cut 15 inches long, so that when they are assembled, there is an approximately 12" X 12" clear opening. (Don't worry about exactitude in the opening. As long as you use the same frame in creating rug sections, they will all fit together.)

When the boards are cut, sand the edges and ends smooth. The frame boards can be painted or sealed for extra smoothness if you like.

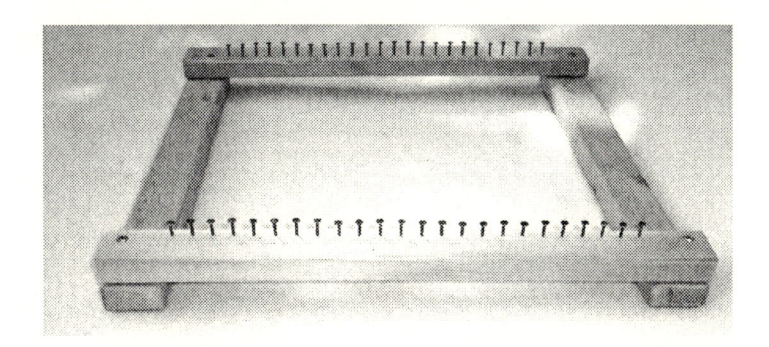

Put the four boards together, just laying the end boards on top of the side boards as shown in the illustration and nail or screw the corners, making sure that the boards are all at right-angles forming a square. Use two screws or nails at each corner so that the frame will hold its shape. The frame in the photograph has one screw in the top board and one in the bottom board at each corner. Only the one in the top board shows.

Finally, add the pegs to the high ends only. In the frame shown, small nails are used, about one inch long (don't use upholstery tacks since they will pull out). If you are using screws or dowels, pre-drill holes so that the boards don't split. You will need 24 pegs on each end, spaced on ½-inch centers. The pegs should be placed about ½ inch in from the edge of the boards. Notice that the pegs line up with the center opening of the frame—don't set the pegs at the ends of the board. As soon as the pegs are set, the frame is ready to use.

Preparing the Warp

A marvelous feature of rugs made on pegged frames is that they have four finished edges as soon as they come off the frame. This is made possible by using a continuous warp—a single strip of fabric is wound around the pegs which forms the internal structure of the rug.

The first warping you will use is a ½-inch warp pattern since the pegs are that far apart. This width of warp is used for all of the rugs in Part I, with the exception of locker hooking.

To begin, you will need your warp fabric prepared. All of the rugs shown use 1½-inch strips of light woven cotton fabric (broadcloth) and the strip is double-folded for smoothness. You can iron in a double-fold or see the Handbook in Part V for how to use bias-tape folders to make the strip. If you don't have the time to make a fabric warp, see the Handbook section on using alternate materials.

The fabric used for the warp won't show on the surface of any of the rugs in Part I of the book, so you don't have to worry if it is an odd color or print. In all of the photographed rugs, you'll notice that the warp is a different color than the fabric being used for the surface of the rug. That is simply to show the process more clearly. The warp fabric and the fabric for the rug surface can be all the same, but there is one practical consideration in choosing a different color for the warp fabric. If you are working on a small frame and will be lacing several sections together for the finished rug, a warp of a different color is just easier to find.

To warp the one square foot frame, you will need about 25 feet (8+ yards) of continuous strip. If you are using a shorter length of fabric, sew the individual pieces together using the regular bias joint illustrated in the Handbook section.

Putting the Warp on the Frame

Wrap the prepared fabric strip around the first two pegs (top and bottom) at one end of the frame. Tie the end of the loop closed. Be sure to tie the fabric strip to the fabric strip—don't include the nail or peg in the knot. Leave about a six-inch tail loose. It will be laced into the rug once it is done.

Making and Warping the Frame 5

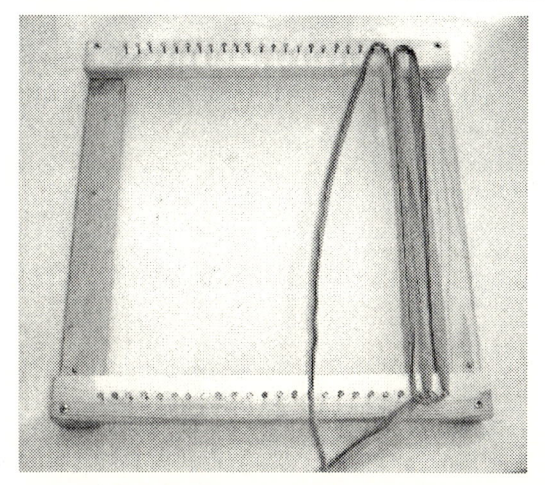

Then wrap, working in a continuous line around two pegs at one end, then two pegs at the other end as shown in the photograph.

Don't skip any pegs and try to keep an even tension (but not pulling tight) on the fabric strip. When you get to the last wrap, there will be just one peg left. Pass the fabric strip around it and tie the loop of warp around the previous pair of pegs. Again, be sure that the peg isn't caught in the knot. There should also be about a six-inch tail of strip left after this last knot is tied.

The warping is now complete and you are ready to begin making your rug.

Note that this same warp can be used for all but one of the rug techniques in Part I. When the instructions refer to a "continuous warp at ½-inch spacing" the above directions will apply.

Warping an Old Frame

Most older frames have wooden pegs spaced on one-inch centers. To apply a ½-inch warp to those frames, the warp strand passes around every peg instead of pairs of pegs. Don't be concerned if the frame has an odd number of pegs, as many older frames do. The illustration below shows a continuous warp on a frame with 17 pegs. With an odd number of pegs, the warp begins and ends at opposite corners, but that does not affect rug making.

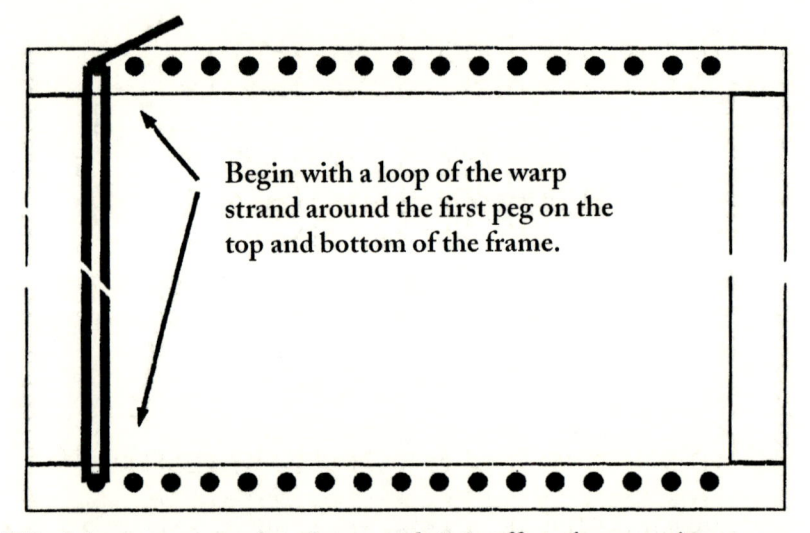

Begin with a loop of the warp strand around the first peg on the top and bottom of the frame.

Wind the warp around each peg and tie it off on the opposite corner.

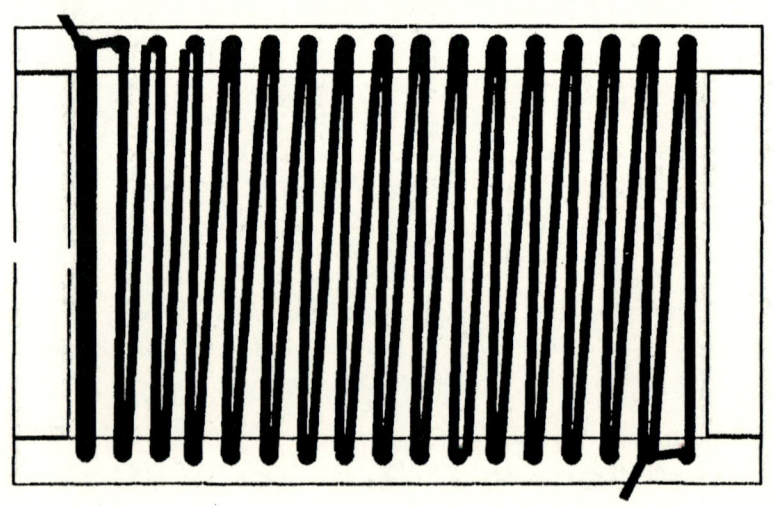

CHAPTER 2
Knotted Shag Rugs

With every book, I always debate which rug should come first. For this book, I settled on a long-time favorite, the knotted shag rug, which I first wrote of in 1986. The technique is very basic and can be done as a family or group project. The most remarkable class project was a kindergarten class in California that made a knotted shag rug for their school fundraiser. Their 2-foot by 3-foot rug sold at their school auction for $300 and not only did the kids have fun, many of the parents and teachers got hooked on making rugs at the same time.

Another reason for beginning with the knotted shag rug is that it can be made with just about any material—in very small pieces—making it an ideal project for recycling clothing. For a soft, easy to care for rug, collect some old T-shirts. For a heavy-duty rug, old blue jeans are good. Light-weight woolens make a resilient rug and sewing leftovers will make a very colorful rug.

Also, the knotted shag rug is one of the easiest rugs to work in a design or pattern. Since the knots are made in rows, you can sketch out a design on paper. Keep the design simple because details won't show.

Have your frame warped with fabric strip following the directions in Chapter 1. (If you don't want to use fabric, see the section on using alternate materials in the handbook.) Cut the fabric for your shag pieces. For most fabrics the shag pieces should be at least three inches long, which will result in a shag height of a little over an inch. For first-time rug makers shag pieces of five or six inches long are the easiest to handle. The rug shag depth will be over two inches but can be trimmed down to the desired height.

- Heavy woven fabrics (like denim or wool) should be cut ½ to ¾ inches wide on the bias (diagonal) of the fabric
- Light woven fabrics (like calico) should be cut or torn 1½ to 2 inches wide on the straight grain
- T-shirt cottons and medium weight knits should be cut 1 to 1½ inches wide
- Lighter knits should be cut about 2 inches wide

Although almost any fabric can be used for the knotted shag, for your first rug avoid very light or slick fabrics. They require special handling as described in the fine points of knotted shags below.

The knots are all made over pairs of the warp strands using a what is called the *weavers knot* which is made in three steps:

- First, lay the shag piece over the first *pair* of warp strands so that it is approximately centered.

- Second, bring the ends of the strip around and under the warp strands, then pull both ends up to the top.

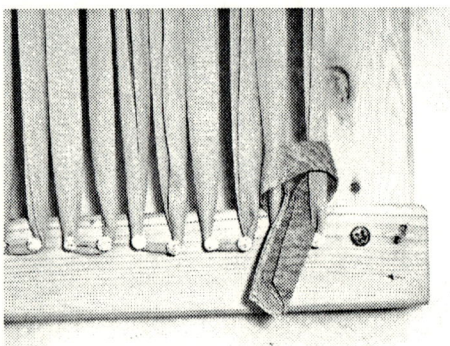

- Finally, pull on the ends of the shag piece to tighten the knot.

The Knotted Shag Rug

Move over to the next pair of warp strands and repeat the process with the next shag piece. Complete the **first row** of knots working over each pair of warp strands in turn. Since there are an even number of warp strands, the first row of knots should cover every strand. Slide the first row of knots down the warp strands so they are next to the pegs on the frame.

For the **second row,** the same knots are used but they are offset by one warp strand (note the offset in the photo above). Skip the first warp strand at the edge and make the first knot over the second and third warp strands. Continue across the row and you should end with one warp strand not covered by a knot at the other end as well.

For the **third row,** begin with the first pair of warp strands again. Knot over *every pair* of warp strands—there shouldn't be any in this row not covered by a knot.

The pattern of knotting continues with each row of knots offset from the previous row. (Alternate the instructions above for the second row and third row.) As you complete each row of knotting, slide the knots down so that they are firmly against the previous row of knots.

These rugs are held together by the tight packing of the rows of knots—not by how tightly each knot is made. It is important to make sure that each row of knots is pushed against the previous row very solidly.

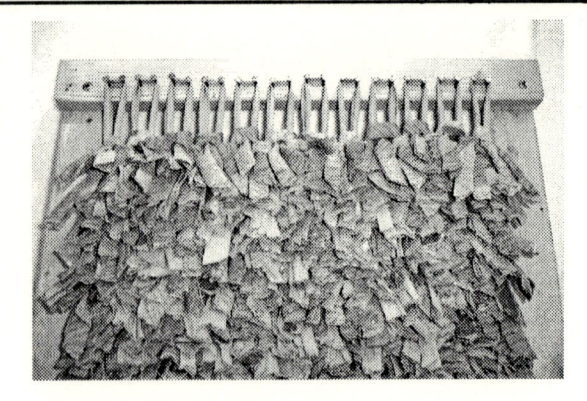

When you get near the row of pegs at the far end of the frame, slide two or three rows of knots up toward those pegs so that the last rows of knotting are not right up against the frame.

When there isn't room for another row of knots, consider the rug done. A small gap between the last two rows of knots is fine—the other knots will adjust themselves on the warp strands and the gap will disappear, if all of the previous knots are packed firmly.

To make sure that the knots are packed together properly, turn the frame over and look at the back of the rug. You should not see exposed warp strands.

The next step is to **remove the rug from the frame**. Use a small crochet hook to catch a loop of the warp at the corner, between two pegs. Pull the warp strip out, away from the rug so that it will come over the pegs. Move to the next warp loop and pull it off and over the next pair of pegs. Work down one side of the frame removing all of the warp strand loops, then turn the frame around and remove the warp from the pegs on the other side. Note that the very first warp loop is the toughest to remove—the rest get easier as the rug is gradually released from the pegs.

The very last thing to do is work the ends of the warp fabric back into the rug. Thread the strip into a large-eye lacing needle or tapestry needle. On the back side of the rug insert the needle through the base of several knots and pull the fabric strip through them. Clip off any excess. You can sew down the end of the warp with a few hand stitches if you want to make sure that it doesn't work loose in the laundry.

The Fine Points of Knotted Shag Rugs

Knots Too Loosely Packed. If you used a very resilient fabric (stiff and/or springy) you may find that they just won't stay packed together and keep springing back. This isn't usually apparent until after the rug is off of the frame, but it isn't a disaster. Working on the back side of the rug, slide several rows of knots toward one end. Over the exposed warp strands, weave in two rows of the same fabric that was used for the shags. Use a simple tabby weave (over one, under one) and work across the warp and back again. Lace the ends of the weaving strip back into the warp.

Push the woven section hard against the knots and then slide several more rows of knots up to the weaving. Repeat the process with weaving over the warp strands. Only do two rows of tabby weave in any one place to avoid getting a thin spot in the rug. The purpose of the weaving is to tighten the warp strands up against the knots and keep them in place. When the knots are so tightly packed that they cannot be slid over the warp strands, the tension is right and no more weaving is required.

Making a Rug without a Nap. In the basic directions for the knotted shag rug, you will find that all of the shag ends lay the same direction. This is called a "nap." If you want a rug without a nap, the direction in which the knots are made is reversed in alternate rows. In the first row, the shag ends are pulled toward the pegs and the second row away from the pegs. The third row is made with the ends pulled toward the pegs again. This is a little harder to do since the ends of the shags in the reversed rows will get in the way of the next row of knots so it isn't recommended for your first rug. Also, this technique should be worked from both ends of the frame working toward the center of the rug.

Working with Very Light or Slick Fabrics. Some light and slick fabrics will require special handling or they will work themselves loose before you can finish knotting a row. If that is occurring, you need to work the knots in opposing pairs as if they were a single knot. Make a knot with the tails facing away from the pegs. Then over the same two warp strands, make another knot with the tails facing toward the pegs. In the general directions above, this pair of knots counts as a single knot. A row of these opposing pairs is the same as a "row of knots" in the directions above.

Adding Extra Fringe to the Sides of the Rug. The shaggy pieces in the knotted shag rugs will generally lay outward forming a shaggy edge. If you want to add more fringes at the sides, it can be done. Using the even number of warp strands in the basic directions automatically creates the points where fringes can be added to the sides of the rugs if desired. In alternate rows, there is one warp strand that is not included in the knotting. Work from the front side of the rug and make one weavers knot over the unused warp strand only. If your knots are packed properly, you will need to use a crochet hook to help place the knot. Insert the crochet hook between the unused warp strand and the body of the rug. Fold a shag piece in half and place the fold over the hook. Pull the loop up above the warp strand. Thread the ends of the shag through the loop and pull on them to tighten the knot. Do not add fringe to the sides of small rugs that will be laced together to form a larger piece.

Joining Small Knotted Shag Sections to Make a Large Rug. The one square foot frame is ideal for rug making, but the individual sections need to be joined to make a large rug. The sections are laced together using the same fabric that was used for the warp (1½-inch strips of woven cotton or blend fabric). This fabric is laced over the warp strands only (never into the knots on the rug). Lay out your rug sections in the order you want them in the rug, arranging them for color, pattern and nap. Make sure that the warp strands in every piece are oriented the same direction, preferably running the length of the rug. Pin notes to each section so that you remember the placement.

Lacing is done from the back side of the rug in rows. For example if your rug will be three squares wide and five squares long, the first step in the assembly is to lace each row of five squares together in order. Pick up the first two squares to be joined and lay them face down on a table.

Thread a large-eye lacing needle or tapestry needle with the fabric strip. Match up the warp loops from the two rug sections. Insert the lacing needle in the first end loop of one square (going down) and then in the matching warp loop (coming back up). This forms one whip stitch with the fabric strip. Pull the lacing strip through, leaving at least a six-inch tail. Repeat the stitch through the same two loops. Move to the next pair of warp loops and make one stitch. Work across to the other end making one whip stitch in each matching pair of warp loops and placing two stitches in the corner pair. Clip off the lacing strip leaving at least six inches of tail. (This process is illustrated in the Handbook section.)

Pick up the next square in the row and repeat the process. All of the squares in the row are joined in the same manner. When one row of squares is laced together, repeat the process with each of the next rows until your rug pieces are all joined into rows.

To lace the rows of squares together, you will be working with the whip stitch again, but the stitches will be placed over the unknotted spaces in the warp on the sides of the sections. Note that those spaces won't be lining up neatly (they never do) so this lacing takes a little more finesse. Make two whip stitches in the corner and one whip stitch on the warp strands of the two pieces, matching them as closely as possible. When you reach the end of the first set of blocks, there should be four corners which line up. If they don't, go back and readjust the placement of the last few whip stitches. Where the four corners meet, place two whip stitches in the aligning corners. These stitches are worked in the loops of warp that form the corners.

Work down the row, matching all corners and placing two whip stitches at the corner. If you run out of lacing strip part way through, make a second stitch with it at that point, leaving at least a six-inch tail. Begin a new lacing strip—also with two stitches and leaving a tail.

When all of the rows of blocks are laced together, use the lacing needle to work the tail ends of the lacing strip into the rug. This is also done from the back, but these tails should be threaded underneath a row of knots working up a nearby warp strand. If you used a fairly slippery fabric, sew the ends of the lacing strips in place with needle and thread so that they can't work their way back out.

High-Speed Knotted Shag Rugs

This method really seems like cheating since there aren't any knots involved, but when you want a shaggy rug in a hurry, it's a good technique to know. Have the frame warped as in Chapter 1 with a continuous ½-inch warp of cotton fabric.

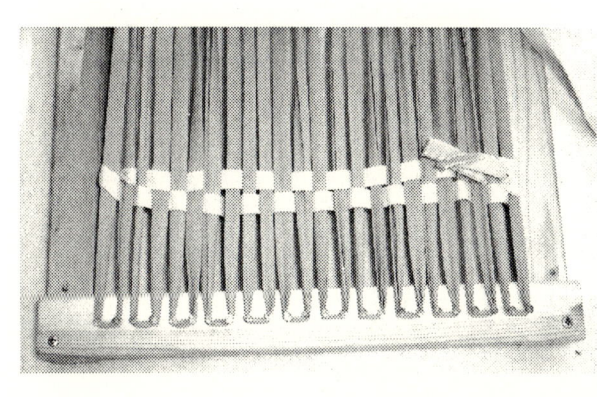

Using the same fabric as for the rug surface (1½-inch cotton is shown) weave two rows of plain tabby about 2 or 3 inches from the pegs. Do not pull the weaving tight. Bring the ends of the weaving strip around the last warp thread and up through the weaving. They will act like added shags. The weaving simply acts as a "keeper" to prevent the knots from loosening. Like the knotted shag, the rows of loops must be packed tightly.

Use a long continuous strip of fabric to save time. (Bulky yarns will also work with this technique, but read the section on using alternate materials in the Handbook.) This method is done just using your fingers.

- Pull a loop of strip between the first and second warps so that it lies underneath the first warp at the outside edge.

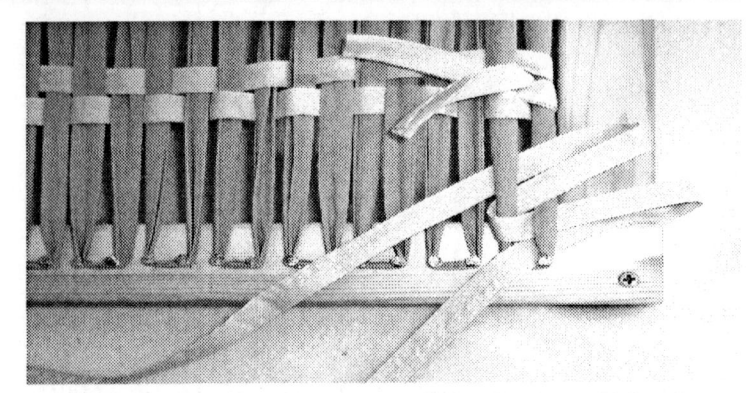

- Holding the first loop in place, pull another loop under the second warp strand so that it lays on top of the first warp strand.

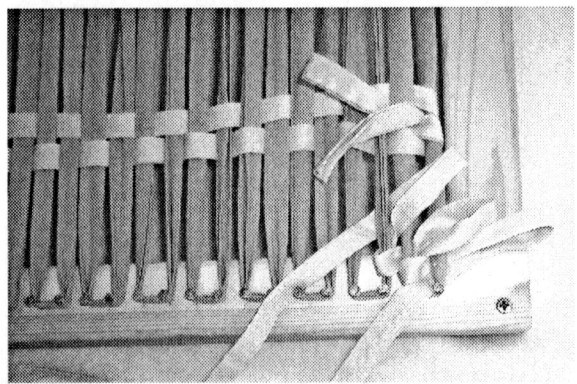

- Holding that loop in place, pull another loop under the third warp strand so that it lays on top of the second warp strand.

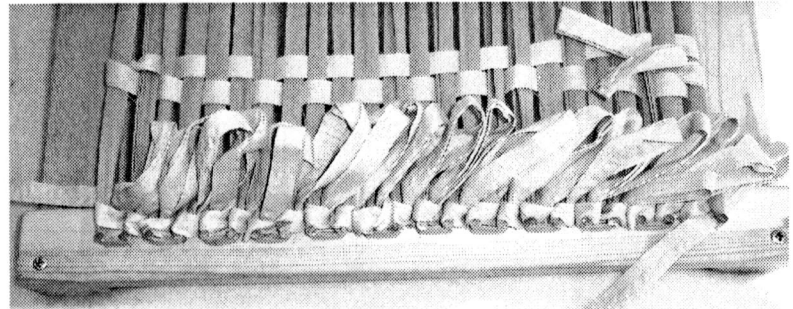

- Repeat with each warp strand in sequence across the row. Push the knots up against the pegs.

The Knotted Shag Rug 17

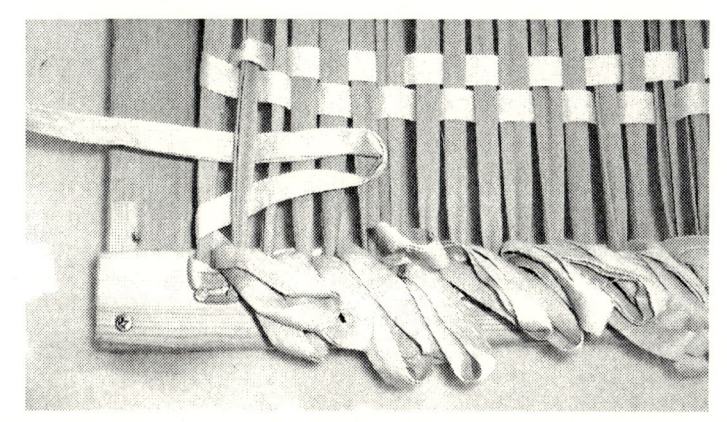

- The second row is worked going the opposite direction. Pull a loop under the first warp strand so that it comes up between the first and the second warps. (Note that the first warp strand is enclosed.
- Then pull a loop under the second warp strand so that it comes up between the second and third warps.
- Repeat the process with each warp strand in turn across the row. When the row is complete, push the knots down firmly against the previous row.
- To begin the third row, working back the other direction, pull a loop under and around the first warp strand and pass in under the second warp strand.
- The next loop is pulled under the second warp and over the third. Then under the third and over the fourth warp strands. Repeat with each warp strand in turn across the row.

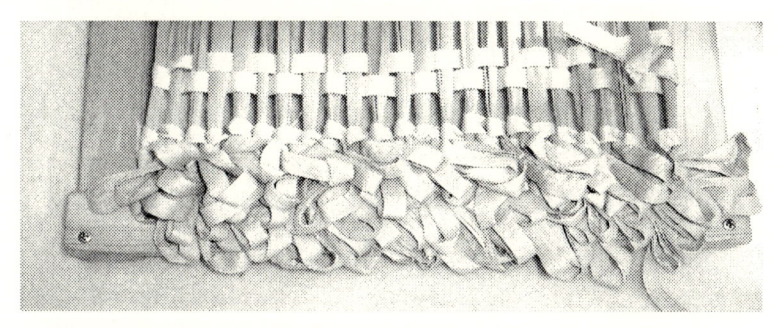

- To make the fourth row, repeat the process in the third row going the opposite direction. Note that the last loop pulled in the third row is really the first loop for the fourth row.

- End the fourth row by clipping the strip at about the shag height. Bring it to the top of the rug around the last warp and under the second warp strand.

- Slide the fourth row down very firmly against the previous rows *and then slide the "keeper" weaving rows down* against it.
- Repeat the entire process above beginning by weaving a pair of "keeper" rows first and then making four rows of loops.

- Make at least one set of four rows with a keeper loop at the other end of the warp also, so that in making the final rows to finish the rug aren't up against the pegs. Or, you can work rows alternately from each end of the frame for a symetrical design.

This rug gets its structure and solidity by tightly packed rows. When you remove it from the frame, if you can detect any looseness in the rows, weave in more keeper rows. The added keeper rows are worked from the back.

The final step in finishing the rug surface is to clip the loops if the rug is going to be used on the floor. I can't say this often enough, but rugs with tall loops are a hazard for tripping and pets can get caught in them. Save the loops for wall hangings only.

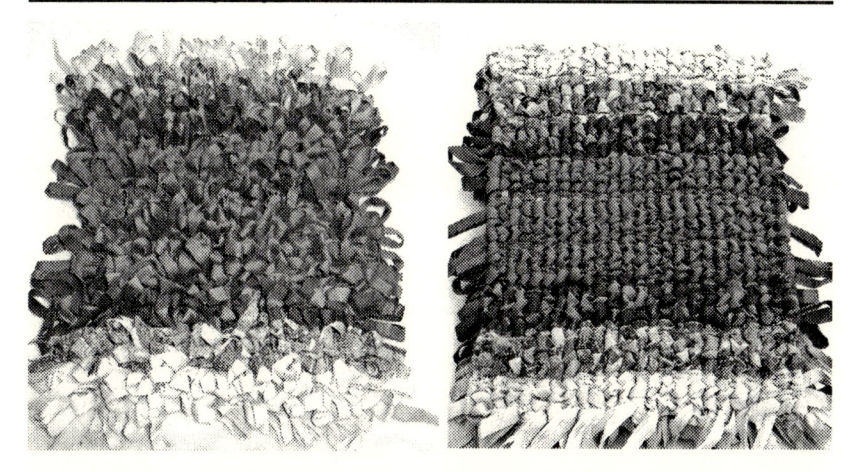

Above is the finished rug after removal from the frame. The top loops (left) have not yet been cut. The back of the rug (right) shows tightly spaced rows with little of the warp strands exposed.

A note to weavers using rug looms: If you've wanted to weave shaggy rugs, but were put off by the time it takes to knot each shag, the high-speed knotted shag is just what you have been looking for. The technique is very adaptable to loom work, with just a couple of modifications.

Close the shed and make a test row of the high speed knots. With a regular cotton rug warp of 8/in and cotton fabric strip, a group of three or four warp strands is counted as one in following the directions above. If you are using yarn for the shag, two warps counted as one are about right, but do a check with whatever material you plan to use.

The rugs are begun just as with any rug and the shaggy portions can be begun at any point. The process, when using a loom, is reversed from the frame since the keeper strands aren't woven first. Instead, with the shed closed, work four rows of knots. Then open the shed and weave two rows of tabby as usual. Close the shed again and add more rows of knots. If you are using a fine weft, additional keeper rows may be needed to keep the shag from overfilling the surface.

CHAPTER 3:
Those Darned Rugs

It isn't often that I darn socks, but while mending a favorite wool pair about 15 years ago, it occurred to me that darning would also make an excellent rug structure. These rugs are good for a first frame rug since they are very simple constructions and can be made with short strips of fabric. The basic directions call for using a strip that will work one entire row across, but shorter strips are fine too.

For a strip long enough to work one row at a time so there is no need for elaborate fabric preparation. An old sheet or piece of cotton fabric (about two yards) can be cut or torn lengthwise into strips. The strips should measure about six times the width of the warp and should be 1½ inches in width. For the one square foot frame, the strips should measure six feet long by 1½ inches wide.

The samples of both techniques are shown using double-folded strip so that the texture is most plainly depicted, but they are just as feasible with unfolded strips. The textures just won't be quite as clean.

Darned rugs are attractive for the beginner since all of the rows can be worked in the same direction. Of course the appearance of these simple rugs is what is the most important. They have an interesting surface appearance and are soft underfoot with more body than a flat weave. These rugs are reversible, but the top and bottom sides on the frame will have different textures.

The two techniques in this Chapter—the Basic Darned Rug and the Figure-eight Rug—are constructed so similarly that the instructions for the two appear together. Following the instructions are the fine points of making these rugs since both types are handled the same way.

How to Avoid "Waisting"

"Waisting" is the bane of beginning weavers everywhere. As their weaving progresses in length, it also grows narrower forming a "waist," as in the photo at the right. The phenomenon happens because the beginner does not allow sufficient slack in the weft (cross threads) and will also happen with frame made rugs.

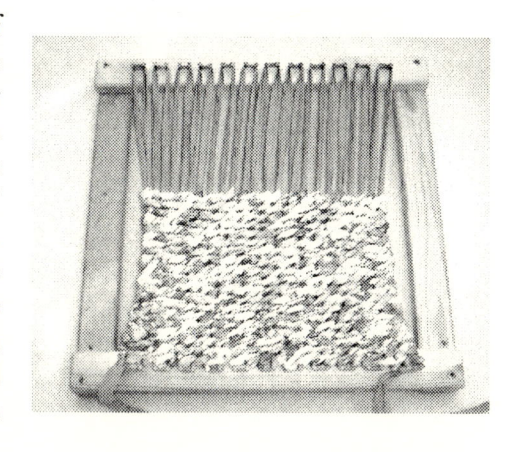

Luckily there is an easy technique to avoid waisting even with non-woven structures. Only the very first row, near the pegs, is worked straight across the warp strands. All of the others are worked on a diagonal or in a gentle curve across the warp, as is shown in the drawing below. Each row is then slid down the warp to its proper position.

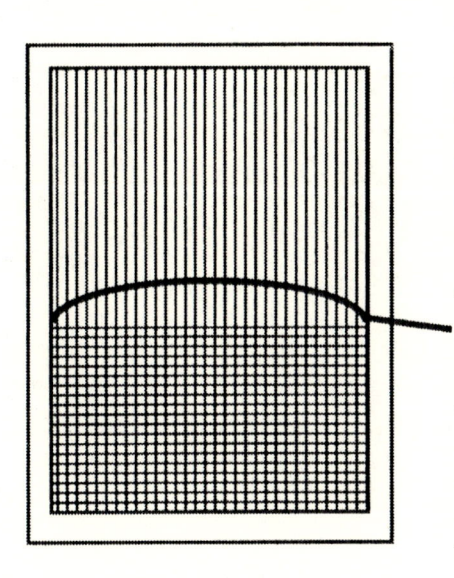

Notice the example of waisting in the photo is made with the basic darned rug construction. If your work (in any of the techniques) begins to look like it, stop and pull out several rows.

Then consciously work at more of a diagonal to keep slack in the work. The structure of all of these types of rugs depends on packing many rows of stitching into the warp strands—it does *not* depend on working tightly with each stitch.

Basic Darned Rug, Worked One Row at a Time

- Begin with a frame that has the continuous warp in place. Thread a lacing needle with a length of strip that is a little more than five times as long as the width of the warp. That length will work one row across and allow for sufficiently long tails to lace back in. For the one square foot frame, the strip should measure about six feet (two yards) long, which allows plenty of length to finish off the row.

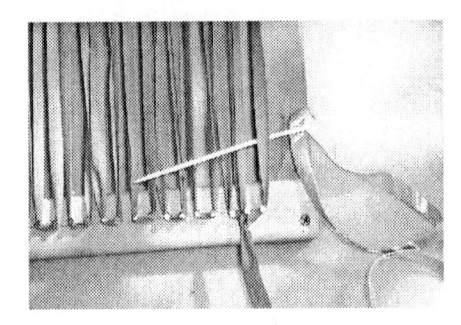

- Pass the needle under the first warp strand only, working from right to left, and bring it back around to the beginning position. Pull through the strip until there is just about a six-inch tail left.

- Pass the needle under the first two warp strands and bring it to the top of the warp.

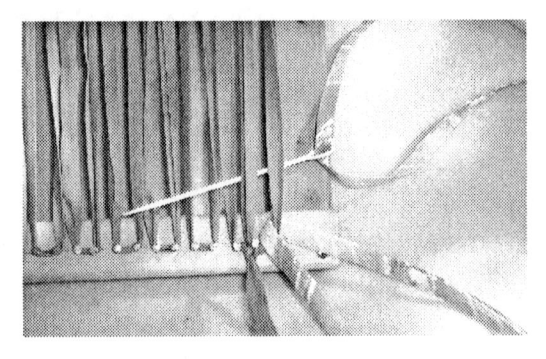

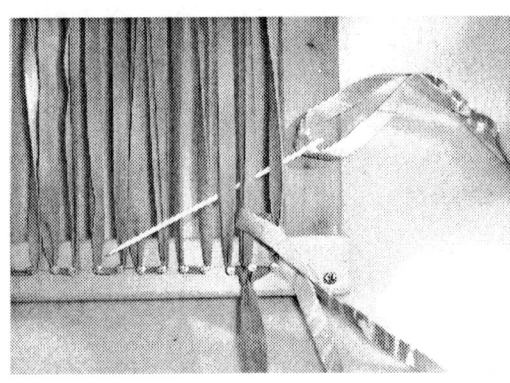

- Bring the needle back (to the right) over the same two warp strands and insert it underneath the next **three** warp strands. Pull through the fabric strip.

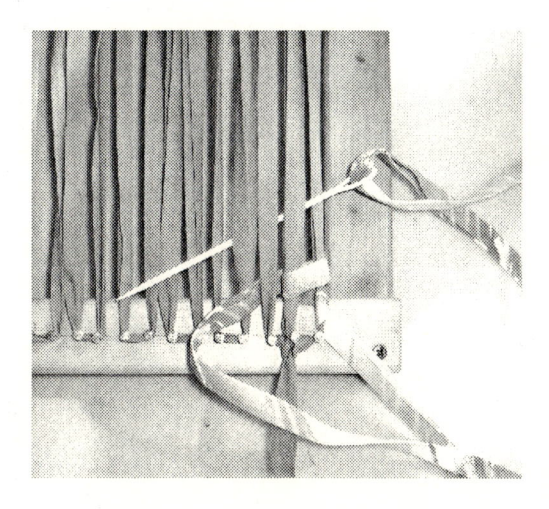

- Repeat this process across the row: Insert the needle two warp strands back (to the right) of where the strip comes up from the warp, then pass the needle under the next three warp strands and pull up the strip. Note that the strip should only be pulled so that there isn't any slack in it. Don't pull it so tightly that the warp strands are pulled out of place. An easy way to get the proper tightness is to put a finger tip between the two warp strands that want to tighten up. Just pull the strip so that the warps are held apart by your fingertip.

- When you reach the end of the row, the final repeat of the sequence will end with the needle inserted "back two" and underneath the last two warp strands. Then go "back one" covering the last warp strand Pull the fabric strip to the outside of the frame. There should be at least six inches of strip left.
- With the strip still on the needle, insert the lacing needle back into the stitches just completed. Pull it under seven or eight stitches and clip off the excess. Do not pull hard on the strip end, since that can also cause "waisting" in the rug.

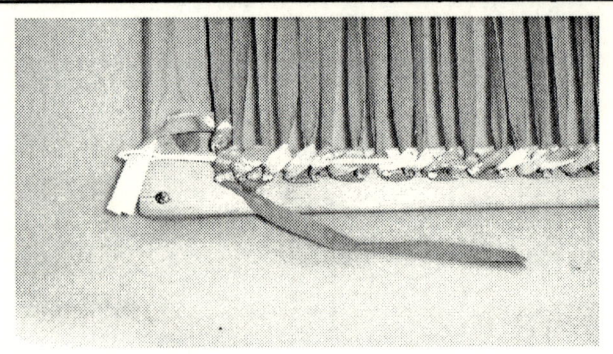

- Go back to the beginning of the row and thread that tail into the needle. Work that strip under seven or eight stitches as well and clip it off.
- Slide the first row up against the pegs.
- The next row is made in exactly the same stitching pattern with a new section of strip. Begin your work slightly away from the previous row and work at a diagonal across the warp strands.

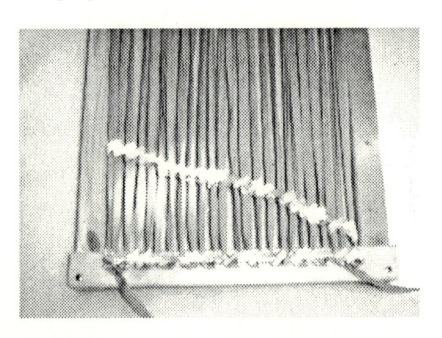

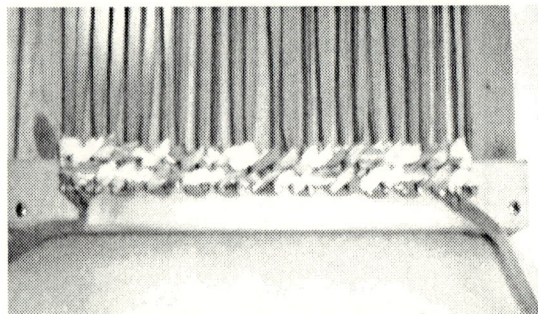

When the stitching is completed and the ends laced in, slide the row up to the previous row and push it firmly in place.
- Continue making rows across and sliding them down the warp each time. When you have almost filled the warp with lacing and are getting close to the pegs at the other end, slide a couple of rows up to the pegs at the other end of the frame. This allows you to darn in the last few rows of the rug a little distance from the frame and the pegs, making the process much easier. Fill in and finish the last few rows, and you are ready to remove the rug from the frame.

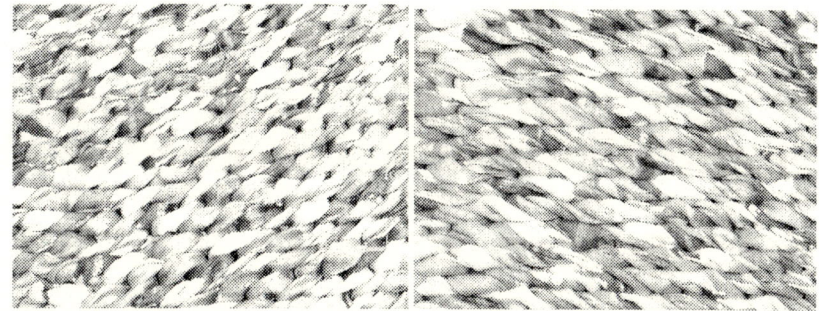

When darned rugs are worked as a series of single rows, all of the loops slant the same direction (have the same "pitch"). Above left is the texture which shows on top of the frame. At the right is the under side.

Basic Darned Rug, Worked Back-and-Forth

This variation produces a slightly different texture since the direction of stitching is reversed in each row. The surface has more of a braided appearance. The advantage to working back-and-forth is that shorter strips of fabrics can be used. Follow the directions above until you nearly run out of your first strip of fabric. Try to leave a tail unworked that is about six inches long. Take the lacing needle off of that strip and thread it with a new strip.

Insert the new strip under six or seven of the last stitches that you made. Bring the tip of the needle up at exactly the same spot that the tail of the old strip is located. Then continue the stitching with the new strip. After making six or seven stitches with the new strip, lace the end of the old strip underneath them. (This doesn't have to be done immediately. You can wait until you have added several strips, then stop and lace them all back into the work at the same time.)

When you reach the end of a row, and have completed the very last "back one," turn the frame over. Begin the new row by inserting the needle under the second warp strand only. Then resume the darning pattern of "under three, back two" working back across the warp.

If the rug is going to see heavy wear and a lot of laundering, you should secure the ends of the tails with a couple of hand sewn stitches with needle and thread. For most fabrics though, the rug materials will mat together a little in use and the ends will stay in place without sewing them down.

After you have completed half a dozen rows of darning, turn your work over and look at the underside of the frame. You probably think the top side looks pretty good, but it is the underneath side which will be the prettiest surface. That is why all of the lacing-in of the ends is done on the top of the rug as you work Of course, both sides of the rug are perfectly usable and attractive, so you should consider it a reversible rug.

When you have almost filled the warp with lacing and are getting close to the pegs at the other end, slide a couple of rows up to the pegs at the other end of the frame. This allows you to darn in the last few rows of the rug a little distance from the frame and the pegs, making the process much easier. Fill in and finish the last few rows.

The Figure-eight Darned Rug

This style of darning is done very similarly to the basic darned rug, but the finished texture is quite different. With the figure-eight, the "best" side is also on the underside as you work. The appearance of the figure-eight will be most prominent with slightly heavier fabrics. The sample rug is made with a polished cotton, but light woolens are also a good choice. If this is the first rug you are making, be sure to read the section on how to prevent "waisting" above.

• Begin with a frame that has the continuous warp in place. Thread a lacing needle with a length of strip that is about six times as long as the width of the warp. For the one square foot frame, the strip should measure about six feet (two yards) long to make sure that there is plenty of length to finish off the row.

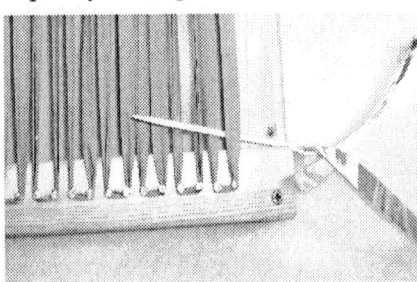

• Pass the needle under the first warp strand only (working from right to left) and bring it back around to the beginning position. Pull through the strip until there is just about a six-inch tail left.

- Pass the needle under the first warp strand, over the second and under the third. Pull the strip up to the top.

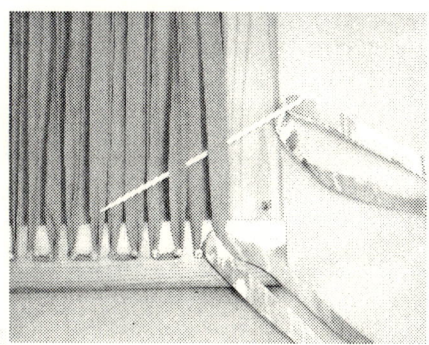

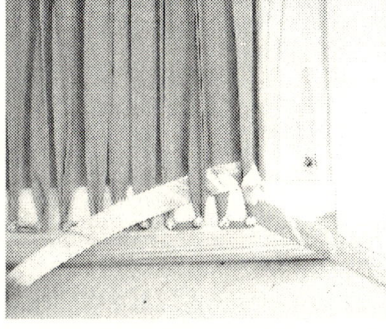

- Bring the needle back (to the right) two warp strands. Pass it under that warp, over the next and under the third. Pull the strip through.

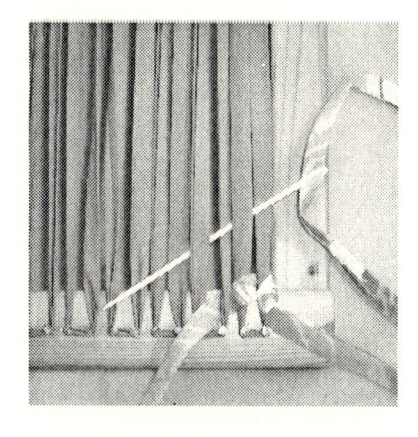

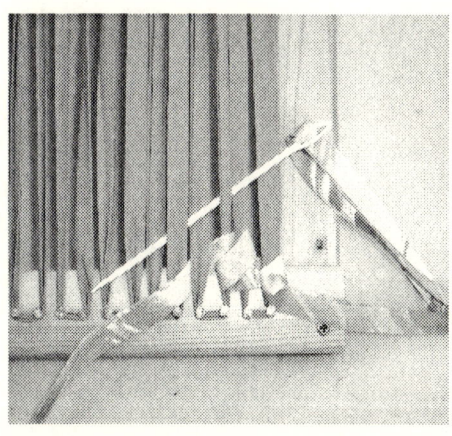

- Repeat this process across the row: Insert the needle two warp strands back (to the right) of where the strip comes up from the warp, then pass the needle under one, over one, under one and pull up the strip. Note that the strip should only be pulled so that there isn't any slack in it. Don't pull it so tightly that the warp strands are pulled out of place.

An easy way to get the proper tightness is to put a finger tip between the two warp strands that want to tighten up, and just pull so that the warps are held apart by your fingertip. (Talk yourself through the process by repeating: "under one, over one, under one—back one.")

- When you reach the end of the row, go "back one" covering the last warp strand. Leave the end of the strip loose—just pulled to the outside of the frame. There should be at least six inches of strip left.
- With the strip still on the needle, insert the lacing needle back into the stitches just completed. Pull it under seven or eight stitches, and clip off the excess.

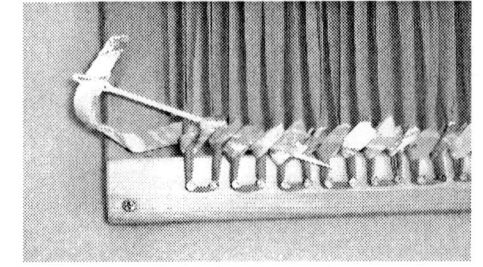

Do not pull tightly when lacing in the tail since that can also cause "waisting" in the rug.

- Go back to the beginning of the row and thread that tail into the needle. Work that strip under seven or eight stitches as well and clip it off.
- Slide the first row up against the pegs.
- The next row is made in exactly the same stitching pattern with a new section of strip. Begin your work away from the previous row and work at a diagonal across the warp strands. When the stitching is completed and the ends laced in, slide the row up to the previous row and push it firmly in place.

If the rug is going to see heavy wear and a lot of laundering, you should secure the ends of the tails with a couple of hand sewn stitches with needle and thread. For most fabrics though, the rug materials will mat together a little in use and the ends will stay in place without sewing them down.

After you have completed half a dozen rows of darning, turn your work over and look at the underside of the frame. You probably think the top side looks pretty good, but it is the underneath side which will be the prettiest surface. You should be able to see the figure-eight pattern that is formed and looks like a row of little bows across the rug. Of course, both sides of the rug are perfectly usable and attractive, so you should consider it a reversible rug.

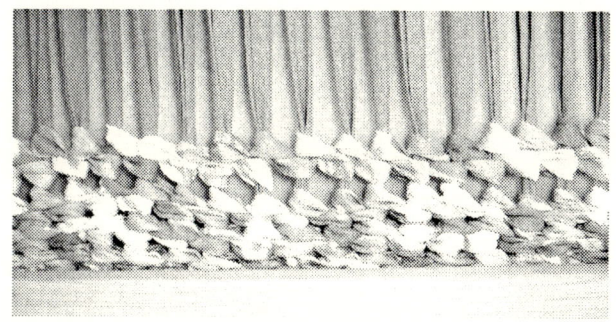

The reverse of the figure-eight darned rug is a series of small bows. Shown above are rows of completed stitching before and after being slid together.

When you have almost filled the warp with lacing and are getting close to the pegs at the other end, slide a couple of rows up to the pegs at the other end of the frame. This allows you to darn in the last few rows of the rug a little distance from the frame and the pegs which makes the process much easier. Fill in and finish the last few rows.

The Fine Points of Darned Rugs

Darning Continuously Back-and-Forth in Rows: Both darned rugs can be made in a continuous fashion by reversing direction at the end of the row and working back to the other side of the frame. In the basic directions above, notice that both techniques begin and end a row with one wrap around the last warp strand. As you come to the end of the first row, make the last stitch around the last warp strand. Then turn the frame over. As you begin the next row, you do not need to begin the row with another wrap around the same warp strand since it is already done.

You will notice that in working back-and-forth in rows that the angle of the stitches showing on the top of the rug are reversed in each row. This is called reversing the "pitch" and gives the top side of the rug nearly a braided appearance. The same reversal will occur on the underside of the rug.

The biggest advantage in working back and forth with darned rugs is that you can easily use odd lengths of fabric strip for the darning—it doesn't have to be long enough to reach completely across one row. If you are making a large rug, this is a tremendous time and frustration saver.

To **change the darning strip in the middle of a row,** simply quit using the "old" strip when there is only about six inches left. Stop at the end of a complete sequence—just before you would go "back two"—and leave the tail of the old strip lying on top of the warp strands. Thread the "new" strip on the needle and insert it seven or eight stitches back in the current row. Bring it out of the stitches so that it is in exactly the same position as the end of the "old" strip. Pull the new strip through the stitches, but don't pull it out of them. Then continue darning with the new strip. When you have completed the row, lace the end of the old strip under seven or eight of the new stitches and clip off any excess.

Because this process is so easy to do, you may be tempted to change strip very often to work in a design. Don't do that! If the strip makes less than 10 stitches, in adjacent rows, you'll be creating a weak spot in the rug. Instead, to work in small designs, see the section on advanced techniques at the end of Part I.

Removing the Rug from the Frame: When the darning is completed, you are ready to remove the rug from the frame. Use a small crochet hook to catch a warp thread at the corner, between two pegs. Pull the warp strip out, away from the rug so that it will come over the pegs. Move to the next warp pair and pull it off and over the next pair of pegs. Work down one side of the frame removing all of the warp, then turn the frame around and remove the warp from the pegs on the other side. Note that the very first warp loop is the toughest to remove—the rest get easier as the rug is gradually released from the pegs.

Finishing the Rug: The only thing left to do to finish the rug is to lace the ends of the warp back into the rug with the lacing needle.

Work them under several rows moving diagonally from row to row. Clip off the end.

Take the rug and set it down on the floor. Notice how differently it looks from when it was on the frame since you are seeing it at a distance. Step on it and notice the built-in springiness. Then put it away somewhere while you make more squares on your frame to complete the rug. For a uniform look in the rug, make more squares of the same materials and using this technique. I know though that there are so many of the techniques here that are just as quickly made (some more so) and with a wide variety of textures. Don't be afraid to make squares of different techniques since as long as you use the same frame with these non-tensioning techniques, they will all fit together to make a "sampler" rug.

Joining Darned Sections to Make a Large Rug. The one square foot frame is ideal for most rug making, but the individual sections need to be joined to make a large rug. The sections are laced together using the same fabric that was used for the warp (1½-inch strips of woven cotton or blend fabric). This fabric is worked over the warp strands only (never into the stitches in the rug). Lay out your rug sections in the order you want them in the rug. Make sure that the warp strands in each piece are oriented the same direction, usually running the length of the rug. Pin notes to each section so that you remember the placement.

Lacing is done from the back side of the rug—which for darned rugs is the same side from which you made the stitches. The rug is assembled in rows. For example if your rug will be three squares wide and five squares long, the first step in the assembly is to lace each row of five squares together in order. Pick up the first two squares to be joined and lay them face down on a table. Thread a large-eye lacing needle or tapestry needle with the fabric strip. These squares should have the end loops of the warp, which will match up between the two squares. Insert the lacing needle in the first end warp loop of one square (going down) and then in the matching warp loop (coming back up). This forms one whip stitch with the fabric strip. Pull the lacing strip through, leaving at least a six-inch tail. Repeat the stitch through the same two loops. Move to the next matching pair of warp loops and make one stitch. Work across to the other end making one whip stitch in each matching pair of warp loops and placing two stitches in the corner pair. Clip off the lacing strip leaving at least six inches of tail.

Pick up the next square in the row and repeat the process. All of the squares in the row are joined in the same manner. When one row of squares is laced together, repeat the process with each of the next rows until your rug pieces are all joined into rows.

To lace the rows of squares together, you will be working with the whip stitch again, but the stitches will be placed between the rows of stitching on the sides of the sections. Note that those spaces won't be lining up neatly (they never do) so this lacing takes a little more finesse. Make two whip stitches in the corner and one whip stitch on the warp strands of the two pieces, matching them as closely as possible. When you reach the end of the first set of blocks, there should be four corners which line up. If they don't, go back and readjust the placement of the last few whip stitches. Where the four corners meet, place two whip stitches in the aligning corners. These stitches are worked in the loops of warp that form the corners.

Work down the row, matching all corners and placing two whip stitches at the corner. If you run out of lacing strip part way through, make a second stitch with it at that point, leaving at least a six-inch tail. Begin a new lacing strip—also with two stitches and leaving a tail.

When all of the rows of blocks are laced together, use the lacing needle to work the tail ends of the lacing strip into the rug. This is also done from the back, but these tails should be threaded underneath the darning stitches working up a nearby warp strand. If you are working with a fairly slippery fabric, sew the ends in place with needle and thread so that they can't work their way back out.

Making Large Darned Rugs in a Single Section: You can make a darned rug of any size by making a larger frame. Keep in mind however that you will need to be able to easily reach the center to make the darning stitches. If you want a rug that is three feet by five feet for example, you will want to be able to work in the narrowest dimension since it is much easier to reach halfway across (a foot and half) of the width than the two and half feet to reach to the center of the length. In order to keep the narrowest dimension available, the pegs are set along the sides of the high/low frame and the warp strands run across the width of the rug. (See the Chapter on the Bess Chet Rug for an illustration of this type of warping. Another advantage of warping from the sides of the frame is that the lines of darning will run the length of the rug allowing for striped designs in that direction.

CHAPTER 4
Amish Knot Rugs

With many of the frame rug techniques, the process is so basic that it has applications in many fields and is called by many names. The Amish Knot construction is also a rug making structure done off of a frame, so I will continue to use that name for it. People who sew will recognize the process as a blanket or buttonhole stitch and former scouts will recognize it as a "half-hitch knot."

This technique is somewhat related to the darned rugs in the previous chapter, but the "good" side of the rug will be on top of the frame as you work, so it isn't easily combined with the darned rugs (unless you want to turn the frame over—and there's no law against that). The Amish Knot forms a raised texture and a thicker rug than the darned rugs so it can be used to accent other flatter textures. If you work pairs of rows of the Amish Knot with different colors the impression is that of a raised braid.

Frame Amish Knot Technique

- Begin with a frame that has the ½-inch continuous warp in place. Thread a lacing needle with a length of strip that is about six times as long as the width of the warp. For the one square foot frame, the strip should measure about six feet (two yards) long, which allows plenty of length to finish off the row.

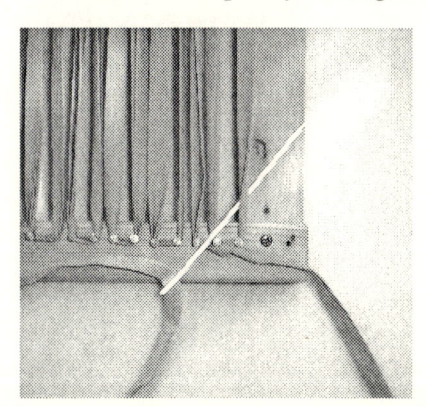

- Pass the needle between the first and second warp strand and bring it to the outside of the frame.

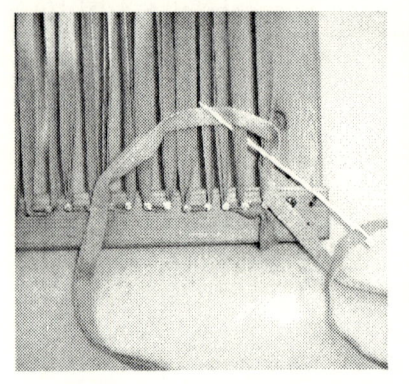

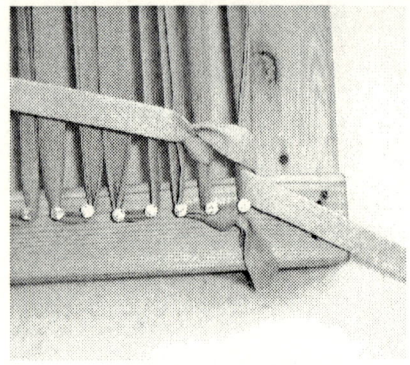

- Hold the working strip on top of the warp. Pass the needle under the second warp strand from right to left. Pull up the strip, allowing a loop to tighten around the working strand. Leave about a six inch tail of strip unworked.
- Insert the needle under the third warp strand moving from rightt to leftt. Pull the strip through, again forming a loop around the stitch. 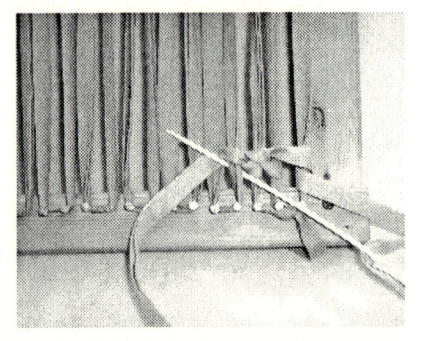
- Repeat this process across the row: Insert the needle under each succeeding warp strand from right to left and pull up the slack. If you always keep the slack in the working strip laying on top of the warp and pinch it in place with your left hand, it should automatically form the correct loop. Note that the strip should only be pulled so that there isn't any slack in it. Don't pull it so tightly that the warp strands are pulled out of place. ("Waisting" is not as big a problem with the Amish Knot rugs as with darned rugs, unless you work maniacally tight knots.)

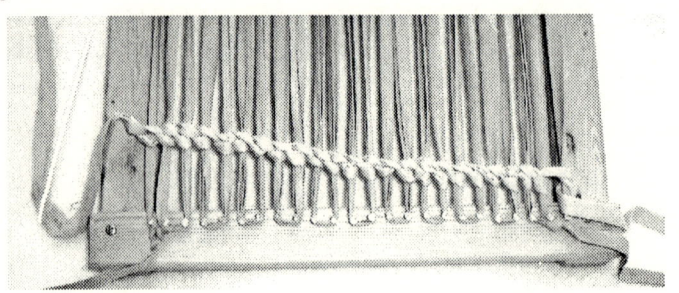

Amish Knot Rugs

- When you reach the end of the row, insert the needle back under the last warp strand, and bring the strip up to the top. There should be at least six inches of strip left.
- With the strip still on the needle, insert the lacing needle back into the stitches just completed. Pull it under seven or eight stitches, and clip off the excess.
- Go back to the beginning of the row and thread that tail into the needle. Work that strip under seven or eight stitches as well and clip it off.
- Slide the first row up against the pegs.
- The next row is made in exactly the same stitching pattern with a new section of strip. Begin your work away from the previous row and work at a diagonal across the warp strands. When the stitching is completed and the ends laced in, slide the row up to the previous row and push it firmly in place.

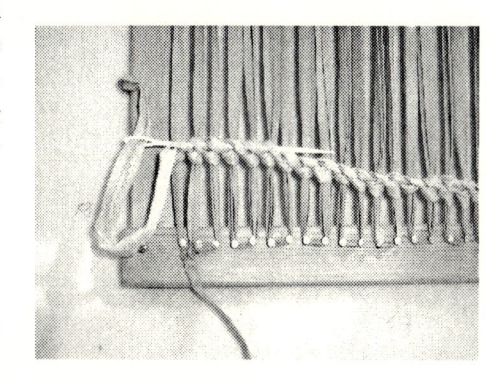

If the rug is going to see heavy wear and a lot of laundering, you should secure the ends of the tails with a couple of hand sewn stitches with needle and thread. For most fabrics though, the rug materials will mat together a little in use and the ends will stay in place without sewing them down.

The Fine Points of an Amish Knot Rug

Working Continuously Back and Forth with the Amish Knot: The Amish Knot is most practical when worked back and forth across the warp in continuous rows. This allows the rug maker to use shorter sections of strip. You have two options for working the knots. The first is to train yourself to make the knots left-handed (or right-handed) so that the frame doesn't need to be turned around. It is easier for most people, however, to simply turn the frame and work back in the direction to which they are most comfortable.

The knotting directions are the same as above with just a single modification. When you reach the end of the warp threads and are ready to work back the other direction, begin the returning row with a knot over the first warp strand.

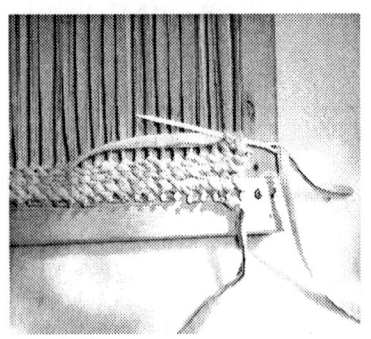

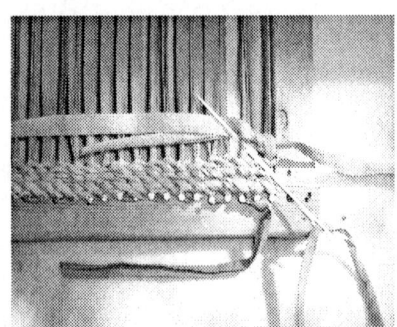

When you run out of one strip, leave at least a six-inch tail loose. Thread the lacing needle with the new strip and lace it under a few existing stitches. Bring the needle out at the same place that the previous strip of fabric ends. Then continue stitching with the new strip. You can change strips at any point except on an outside warp strand. If you do run out of strip at the end of a row, end the row as in the general directions and begin the next row also following the general directions above.

Removing the Rug from the Frame: When the knotting is completed, you are ready to remove the rug from the frame. Use a small crochet hook to catch a warp thread at the corner, between two pegs. Pull the warp strip out, away from the rug so that it will come over the pegs. Move to the next warp pair and pull it off and over the next pair of pegs. Work down one side of the frame removing all of the warp, then turn the frame around and remove the warp from the pegs on the other side. Note that the very first warp loop is the toughest to remove—the rest get easier as the rug is gradually released from the pegs.

Finishing the Rug: The only thing left to do to finish the rug is to lace the ends of the warp back into the rug with the lacing needle. Work them under several rows moving diagonally from row to row. Clip off the end.

Insetting a Design in an Amish Knot Rug: One of the nice features of the Amish Knot is its stability on the warp threads. (It isn't easily slid along them.) This allows for sections of the rug to be worked at different times. Sketch an outline of the area you want to work directly on the warp strands using a permanent marker. Then work back and forth continuously to fill in that area. The lines of knots do not need to be horizontal, but if you do include diagonal lines, watch that there is enough space between the knots to keep the warp strands from drawing together which can create a "waist" problem.

When the design area is filled in, continue with the regular technique in horizontal lines to fill in the background. When turning at the end of a row that touches the design, insert the strip into the filled area so that it just catches the first warp strand in the filled part. Then work back with regular knots.

For vertical lines in a design (like the duck's tail in the photo) make a series of knots along a single strand of warp. When filling in the background around a vertical line, work knots right up to the knotted strand. Pass the needle underneath the knots (between the knots and the warp) and continue across the row as if the vertical knots weren't there.

For more information about working designs in rugs, see Chapter 8 on advanced techniques. The Amish Knot combines well with any of the other non-tensioning rug methods and small squares with central designs make an interesting rug design similar to blocks in a quilt.

Seed Corn Rugs

This variation of the Amish Knot I am including here just as a matter of completeness. This technique creates two knots with each stitch—one around the warp strand and one between the warp strands, more or less resembling the rows of corn on a cob (hence the name). I really don't recommend this stitch for a full rug, since it is tricky as all get out and takes a lot of practice to get the knots with even size and tension. It will, however, add another textural option for a combination rug that you may want to do.

The seed corn stitches also require a needle with a smaller eye than some lacing needles have. The eye needs to be the same diameter as the shaft of the needle. Use a steel lacing needle like the one shown in the photographs or a large size tapestry needle.

- With the fabric strip threaded on the needle, insert the needle between two warp strands (anywhere on the warp) and bring it to the outside of the first warp strand.

- Insert the needle under the second warp strand.

- Twist a loop over the end of the needle and hold tension on the loop so that it does not loosen. For you knitters, this loop is twisted onto the needle just as you would cast on a stitch to a knitting needle.

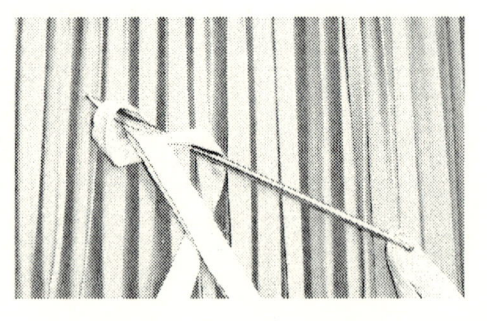

- Pull the needle and the strip through the loop, holding onto the loop the whole time. Snug down the knots.

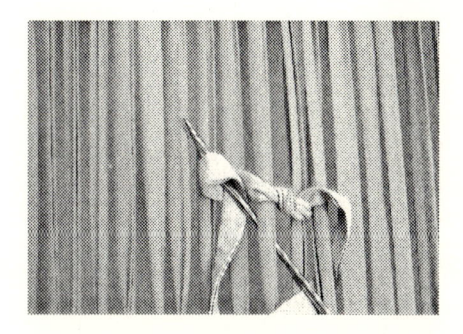

- Insert the needle under the third warp strand, twist a loop over the end and repeat the process.

Practice the stitches until you can make uniform knots each time before using the seed corn technique in a rug. Short strips can be used adding them similarly to the regular Amish Knot, but threading the ends of the strips back into the rugs is done from the back of the rug instead. Lace the ends into the rug along a warp strand, under succeeding rows of knots.

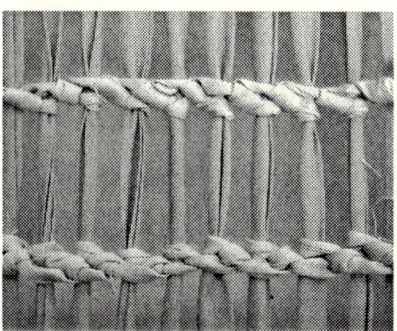

The most pronounced corn-row effect is created when the rows of knots are all worked back-and-forth in opposite directions creating a high and a low line of knots.

CHAPTER 5
Bess Chet Rugs

Like many basic textile methods this technique is called by many names by different specialties. Weavers will recognize this as a "chained weft" while crocheters will call it a "slip stitch" and specialists in embroidery will call it "tambour" work. However, around here the basic method has become known as the "Bess Chet" rug.

There is a small group of my (sometimes willing) testers-of-directions. A while back, this technique came in front of them and I'd asked how they liked it. Unanimously, the method was thought to be easy, quick and readily learned. "Yes," I agreed. "It is one of the best yet."

Knowing the sort of arcane trivia that I have stored in my head, one of them responded, "Okay, but who is Bess Chet?"

Needless to say, the name stuck. The author of the title wishes to remain anonymous (no sense of humor), so I promised I wouldn't reveal that, but I did have to explain where the name came from.

Whatever you want to call it, this rug is one of the best for beginning rug makers. It is easy to learn and makes up quickly. The resulting rug is thick and springy underfoot. It can be made just as easily on a large frame as a small frame since the stitches slide readily along the warp. That also makes it a good technique for inset designs and freeform shaping (see Chapter 8).

The only drawback to the Bess Chet rug is that it requires long strip sections to work efficiently. Prepare woven cottons by cutting or tearing them 1½ inches wide and then stitching them into a continuous length. For unfolded strip join the strips using the overlapping bias joint. For strips that will be double folded, use the regular bias joint before folding. Both joinings are described in the Handbook section. Have your strips rolled into a ball.

Warp the frame with the ½-inch continuous warp using 1½-inch woven cotton fabric. Select a large crochet hook to use. I will be showing the use of a size Q "Handy Hook" brand, but any large hook will work. The stitches made are not sized according to the hook as in regular crochet—instead it is the weight of the fabric strip itself that will determine the stitch size. If you are an experienced crocheter, for heaven's sake don't work tightly. These are supposed to be relaxed loops, which allow the fabric to lay naturally flat. You may even find that it is easier to work this technique without a hook, just using your fingers.

The ball of strip is fed from underneath the frame. You can work with one hand under the warp, or grasp the strip through the warp strands. Don't try to stitch in absolutely straight lines—remember that the stitches will slide along the warp to the position you want.

- With the fabric strip underneath the warp, bring the strip end up to the outside edge of the first warp strand. Tie a slip knot on the crochet hook.

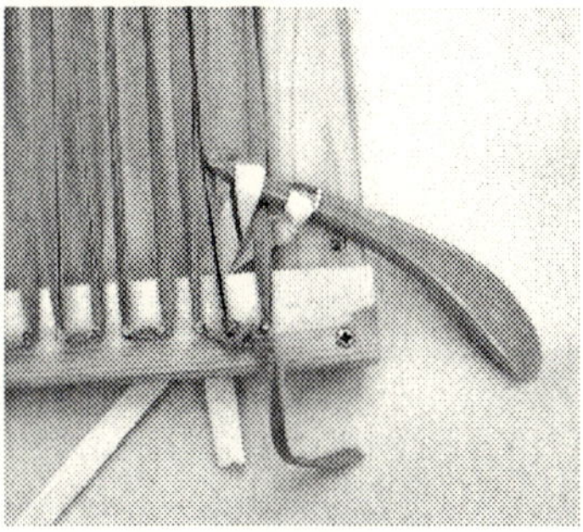

- Insert the hook between the first and second warp strand and pull up a loop of the fabric strip. There will be two loops on the hook.

- Pull the loop just drawn up through the loop on the hook. Only one loop remains on the hook.

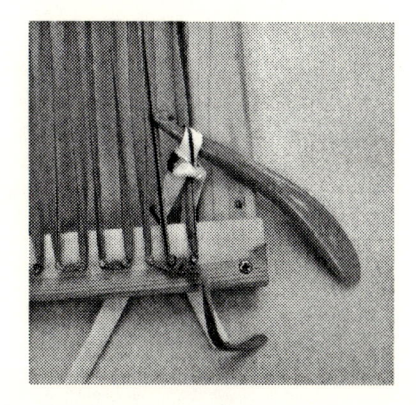

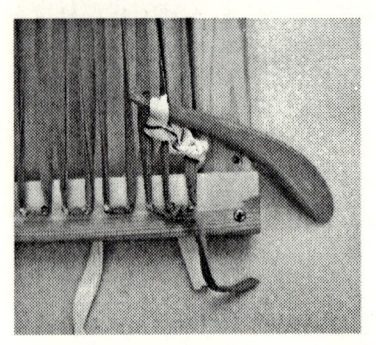

- Insert the hook between the second and third warp strand and pull up a loop of the fabric strip. Then pull that loop through the one on the hook.

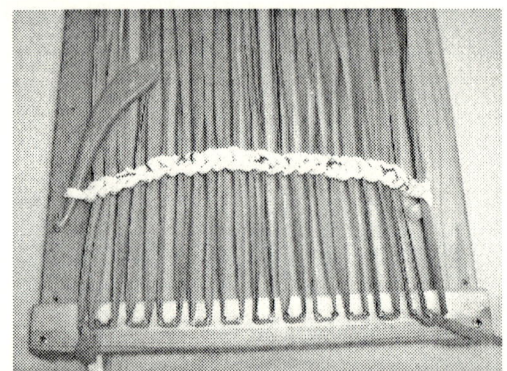

- Proceed across the warp in the same way, pulling up a loop between each set of warp strands, then pulling that loop through the one on the hook.

- When you reach the final warp strand on the other side, pull up a loop just past it and pull that loop through the one on the hook.

- That finishes the first row. Slide the stitches into position. In the photo, the first row is shown slid up to the end pegs. If you are making a large rug, and working the center section first, the rows of completed stitching will be slid toward the center of the frame instead.

- You'll then begin to work back the other direction inserting the hook between the outside warp strand and the next one. The second row is completed and then slid along the warp strands into position.

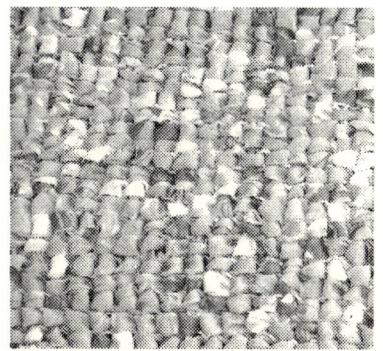

The Bess Chet has distinctly different textures on the front and back of the rug. Above left is the side which will show on the top of the frame. At right is the texture which is created on the under side of the frame. Both sides are attractive on the floor and usable.

The Fine Points of the Bess Chet Rug

To make **a neat chain** always keep the hook pointed in the same direction when making every stitch in the row (always hold the end toward the pegs or away from the pegs). If you want to disguise the chain stitches, alternate the direction the hook is pointed as you draw up the loops of fabric strip.

To **change to a new ball of strip**, stop stitching with the "old" strip when there is at least six inches of strip left. Then, begin the next stitch with a loop of the "new" strip also leaving a tail of about six inches unworked. After making several stitches with the "new" strip, use a lacing needle to lace the tails underneath the stitches.

Small design elements can be worked with short pieces of strip. Begin at any place on the warp with a slip stitch on the hook. Make the stitches in straight, diagonal or circular rows, but don't work more than two sequential stitches over the same warp strand. When the design area is filled in, pull about six inches of the strip up through the last stitch and lace it into the filled area. Also lace the tail from the original slip knot into the design area. (See Chapter 8 for more information about designs with non-tensioning techniques.)

There are two ways of **handling the frame** while making the Bess Chet. If you are strongly right- or left-handed, it will probably be easiest for you to rotate the frame with each row. If you aren't, the most natural way of holding the frame is with the warp threads in a horizontal, rather than vertical position. With the frame in that orientation, the rows are worked away from the rug maker and then back toward the rug maker.

The basic Bess Chet rug has two perfectly usable sides, but the textures are not identical. The back side of the Bess Chet will appear to be woven. If you want to make a **fully reversible rug**, you will need to work with two balls of fabric strip, one on each side of the warp. In one row, work with the standard method above using the strip held below the warp. For the next row, turn the frame completely upside down and work the row using a fabric strip that is on the opposite side of the warp (what would be the top of the warp if the frame were right side up).

Like all of the non-tensioning techniques in Part I, the Bess Chet and its relatives rely on many **rows packed tightly** along the warp for its strength. Always slide a completed row up solidly against previous rows. As the warp is close to filling up, it is easiest to work a few rows next to the pegs on the other end so that the final rows of stitching are away from the pegs.

With a Bess Chet rug, there is a **"turning loop"** at the end of any row if you are working back and forth. These loops are automatically ideal for inserting fringes or as the base for a slip stitch border. Alternately crochet a slip stitch into a turning loop, then chain one stitch. Slip stitch into the next turning loop and chain one. At the ends of the rug, the slip stitches are worked into the warp loops with a chain stitch between. From the slip stitch and chain border additional rows of crochet stitches can also be added.

When lacing together individual sections of the Bess Chet, the turning loops as well as the warp strands are worked with the lacing. If you are joining a Bess Chet section to a rug made with another technique, lace through the warp strand and the turning loop alternately on the Bess Chet only. The lacing procedure applies for all of the rugs in this chapter that are related to the basic Bess Chet.

The Raised Bess Chet Technique

This variation of the basic Bess Chet technique takes off from its roots in crochet. The structure is that of a single-crochet stitch but will not feel natural to anyone with experience in crochet since the working strand is held below the warp and each stitch is worked around two warp strands. This technique is absolutely compatible with the basic method and can be used in conjunction with it to create alternately high and low sections in a rug with the same surface texture.

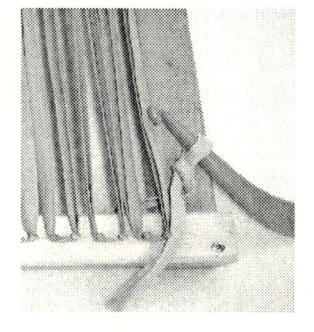

- Have the ball of fabric strip underneath the warp strands. Bring the end of the strip up between the warp and the frame on one side. Make a slip knot over the hook.

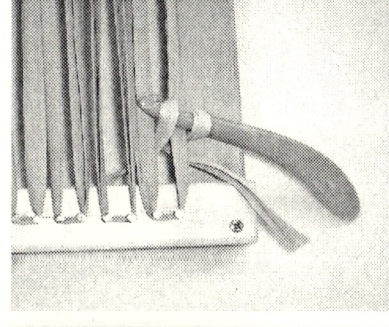

- Insert the hook between the first and second warp strands and pull up a loop. There will be two loops on the hook.

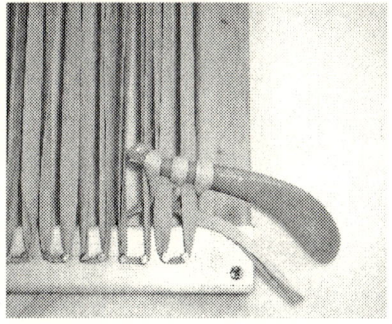

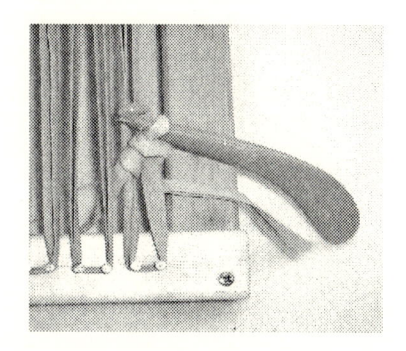

- Insert the hook between the second and third warp strands and pull up a loop. Then pull that loop through the two loops on the hook.

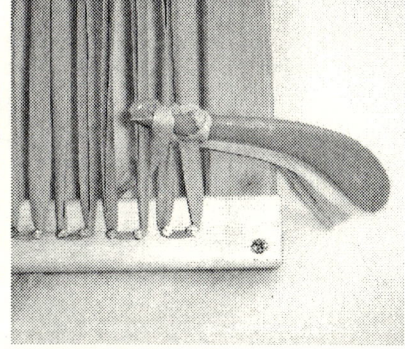

- For the next stitch insert the hook *again* between the second and third warp strands and pull up a loop (two loops on the hook). Notice that this is the same place that the last loop of the previous stitch was drawn up.

- Then insert the hook between the third and fourth warp strands and pull up a loop (three loops on the hook). Complete the stitch by pulling the last loop through the other two.
- Complete the row using the same procedure. Draw up a loop in the same place as the previous stitch ended. Then draw up a loop over the next warp strand, and pull the third loop through the other two on the hook to complete the stitch.
- The last stitch in the row is completed over the last warp strand.
- The next row is begun by turning the frame around (or just working back in the other direction) using the same procedure.

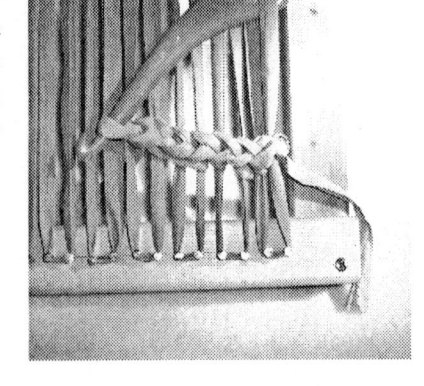

In changing to a new ball of strip or working small areas for design, use the same procedure as for the regular Bess Chet above. Note that you can switch between the two stitches in the same row for alternating high and low areas.

The Tambour Bess Chet Technique

This variation of the basic Bess Chet technique is related to its roots in tambour work. This is the most difficult of the three methods since it is worked with two strands—one held below the warp strands and one held above the warp—and the tension on both strands needs to be about equal so that the braid pattern comes out evenly. (The structure of this method is the same as a two-strand raised tambour braid.)

Because this braid takes some practice to do well, for your first project use two different colors of strip. That gives you a visual clue about which strand is held in which position. In the photo sequence, the darker strand is the one held underneath the warp strands and the light strip is held above the warp. Use a large crochet hook to work the two strands.

You will need two balls of prepared strip. This braid does not work easily with short strips.

- With the dark strip pulled up to the edge from underneath the warp, make a slip knot on the hook.

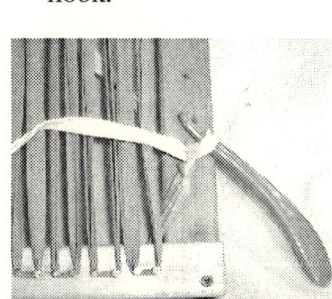

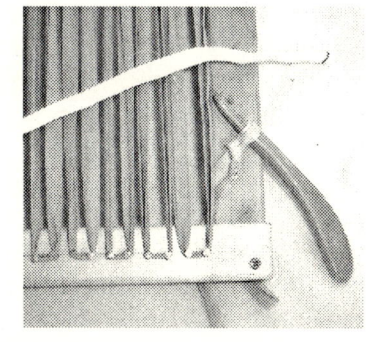

- Pull through a loop of the light strip from above the warp.

- Insert the hook between the first and second warp strands and pull up a loop of the dark strip. Then pull that loop through the loop of the light strip on the hook.

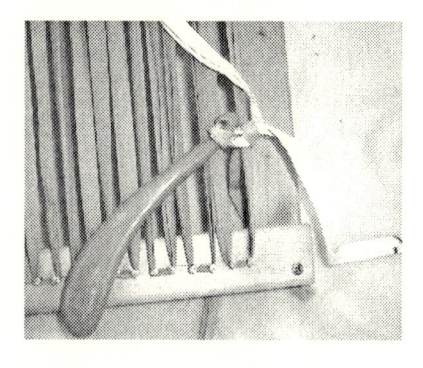

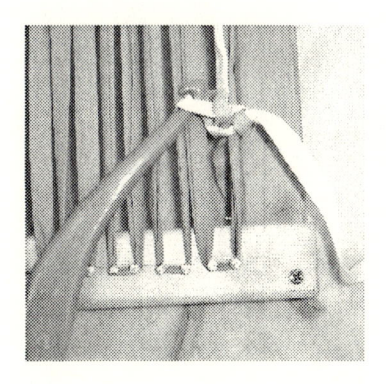

- Pull a loop of light strip through the loop of dark strip on the hook.

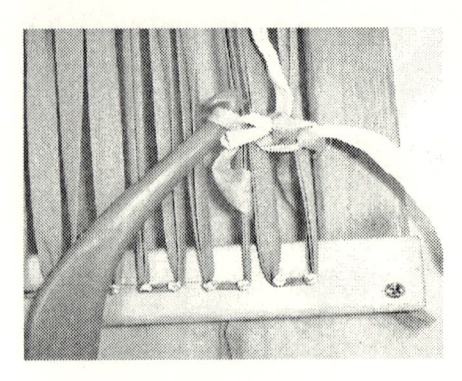

- Insert the hook between the second and third warp strands and pull up a loop of the dark strip. Then pull that loop through the loop of the light strip on the hook.
- Continue in the same way across the warp. Pull a dark loop up in the next space between warp strands and pull it through the light loop on the hook. Then pull a loop of the light strand through the loop of the dark strand on the hook.
- The last stitch of the row is completed over the last warp strand and ends with a light loop on the hook.
- Rotate the frame and work the next row back in the same manner.
- To end a section of stitching, pull about six inches of the strip from the top of the warp up through the loop of the strip from underneath. Clip the upper strip off and lace it under the braid. Then clip off the strip from underneath the warp about six inches long and also lace it under the stitches.

This technique creates a much thicker surface that the other related Bess Chet rugs, but the back appearance is quite similar. In the photographs, the top texture of the raised braid is shown. The lower photo shows the reverse of the tambour Bess Chet, which is quite similar in appearance to the other variations of the technique. (All three rug types will have a flat, almost woven appearance on the reverse of the rug.)

The tambour braid can be used in the same rug as the other two for a special effect, or as a raised border. It can be worked in designs as well (see Chapter 8).

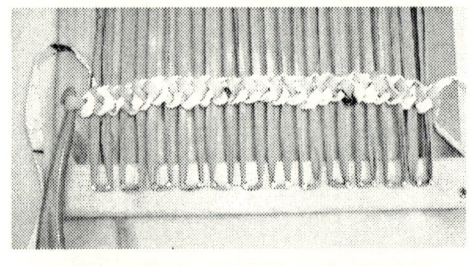

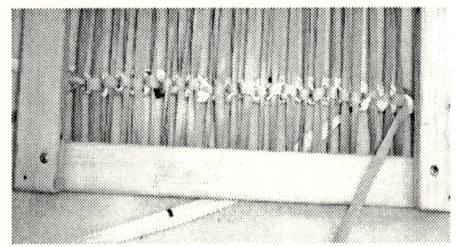

CHAPTER 6
Twined and Needlewoven Rugs

Twined rugs in this chapter use two strands simultaneously to form the rug surface, with each strand wrapped around the warp in turn. The method works best with a slightly heavier fabric that will fill evenly in the ½-spacing of the warp strands. The sample uses a decorator polished cotton cut 1½ inches wide and double-folded to show the texture. If you use light cottons (like calico or broadcloth) cut or tear the strips about 2 inches wide.

The biggest problem with twined rugs and their relatives is that they are prone to "waisting" on a warp with fixed spacing (see Chapter 3). Waisting is most likely to occur when the materials are too thin or light for the rug surface. If you are going to use light material (or yarn), it is best to use an alternate warping technique, such as the scroll frame warp.

The base methods of twining have been well documented and explored by Bobbi Irwin in her book "*Twined Rugs*" so I will be only covering them very lightly. If you would like to learn more about those methods, I would refer you to her book.

Twining is non-tensioning so the technique can be combined with any of the other rug making techniques in part one. The ½-inch continuous warp is used for the rugs in this chapter.

Basic Twining

The structure of twining is of two weft strands twisted around each warp strand. While you are learning this technique it is preferable to use two strands of different colors so that you can keep track of the wrapping. Start with fairly short lengths of fabric strip (around three or four feet) since the full length of the strands has to be pulled through the warp with each wrap.

- Use a safety pin to secure the two working strands together, just outside the warp. One working strand will begin underneath the warp and the other on top of the warp.

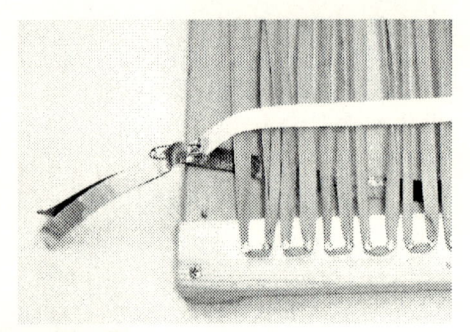

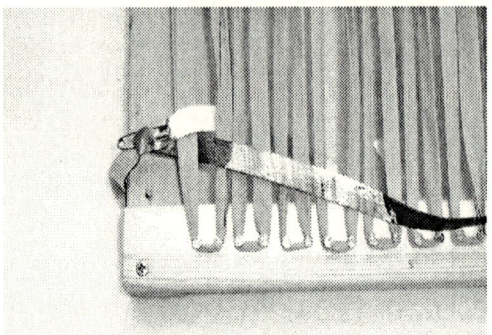

- Bring the strand from the underside up to the top between the first and second warp strands.
- Take the strand from the top and pass it to the underside of the warp, also between the first and second warp strands.

Note that the two working strands "enclose" the first warp strand.

- Bring the strand from underneath up between the second and third warp strands so that it also passes under the working strip on top.
- Take the working strip from the top to the underside of the warp. Notice how a twist is formed around the second warp strand.

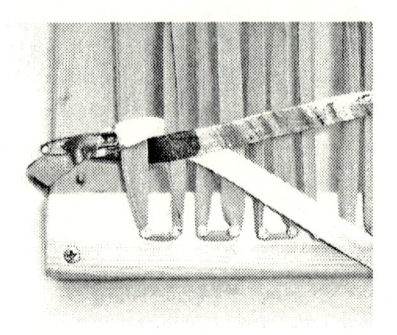

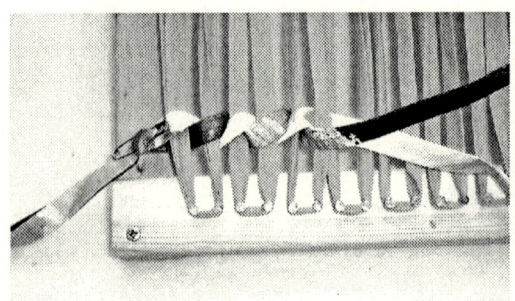

- Bring the strip from underneath the warp up to the top between the third and fourth warp strands and position it so that it crosses underneath the strip on top of the warp.

Twined and Needlewoven Rugs

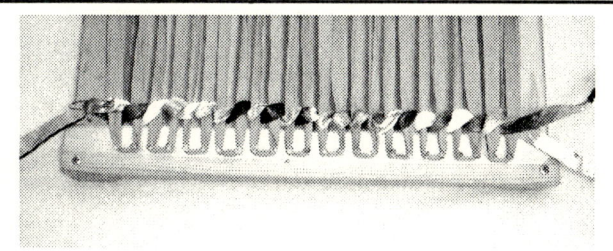

- This process is repeated across the row, working the two strands alternately so that each warp strand is enclosed by the two strands crossing over each other. (Note that in the photographs, the work is shown more loosely than it should be done just to illustrate the process.)

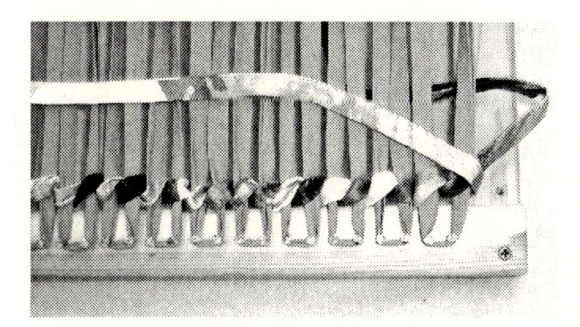

- When you reach the end of the row, the working strips are crossed over the last warp strand and you can work back in the opposite direction (or turn the frame around). If you always keep the twists around the warp strand going in the same direction they will line up from row to row. You can vary the appearance of basic twining by twisting the strips in the opposite direction in alternating rows.

You may have noticed how similar the surface appearance of twining is to the darned rugs in Chapter 3. Because of their similarities, twining can be handled in much the same way as the darned rugs: working single rows straight across; working back and forth; adding on strip; and so forth. Rather than repeat all of that information here, I will refer you to the section on the fine points of darned rugs.

Also note that twining has the same potential for "waisting" as the darned rugs and each row should be worked away from the previous row at a slight angle to prevent that problem.

Twining can also be done with three or more strands if you are adventurous. Refer to Bobbi Irwin's "*Twined Rugs*" for more information on those variations.

Needlewoven (Shortcut Twining Worked Straight)

This technique is a little deceiving. It looks quite simple—yet there are three different surface appearances that can result from minor differences in handling the wefts. For that reason, it can be frustrating for the beginner, so I would recommend practice with the related darned rugs before trying this one. Once you get the hang of needlewoven rugs though, they do make up more quickly than twining.

The standard ½-inch continuous warp is used and like "real" twining, there are two weft strands to handle but they aren't twisted around the warp. Instead, this is a procedure that more closely resembles weaving. You are doubtless familiar with the tabby weave where a weft strand goes over one warp strand and under the next across the row. The needlewoven technique also uses this over one, under one, but with a difference. The working strip goes over one warp strand and then under a second (weft) strip held underneath the warp.

Because of the procedure used, the fabric strip to be held under the warp should be in a long continuous strand. It never needs to be cut unless you want to change colors. The upper strip of fabric is used in short sections—four or five feet with a lacing, weaving or tapestry needle.

- Position the two fabric strips as follows: a ball of continuous strip under the warp strands and a five foot section of the second fabric above the warp strands. Use a safety pin to secure the two strips together just outside the first warp strand. Leave about six inches of strip beyond the safety pin for working in later. Thread a lacing needle with the shorter strip.

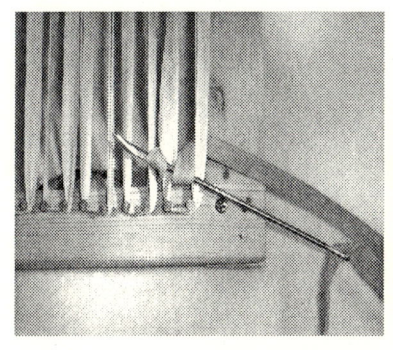

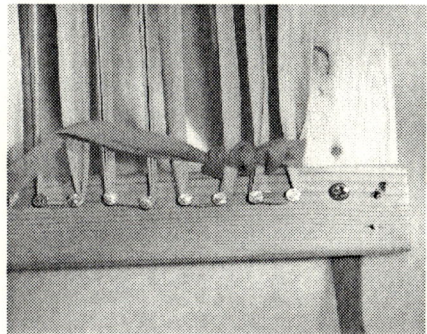

Twined and Needlewoven Rugs   53

- Insert the lacing needle between the first and second warp strands and pick up the weft strip from under the warp. Bring the tip of the needle up to the top so that it will pass over the second warp strand. Then pass the needle under the weft underneath the frame, and over the third warp strand. Pull the needle through the loops and snug down the stitches. 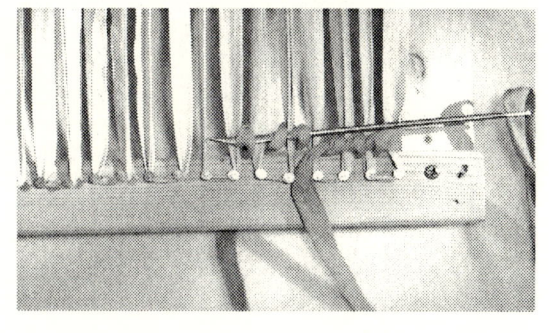
- Pass the needle into the next warp space and pick up a loop of weft from underneath. Repeat in the next and the next warp spaces until there are three (or more) loops on the hook. Pull the needle through the loops and snug the stitches.

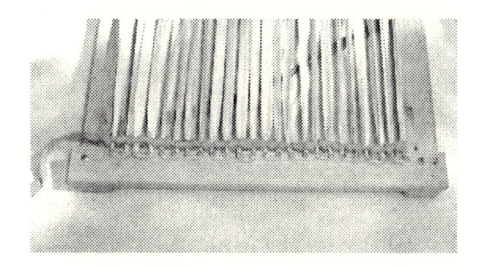

- Continue across the row, going under the lower weft and then over the next warp strand.

Note that for this basic needlewoven texture, the needle always points the same direction as it passes under the weft strand held below the frame. This results in an even rug surface.

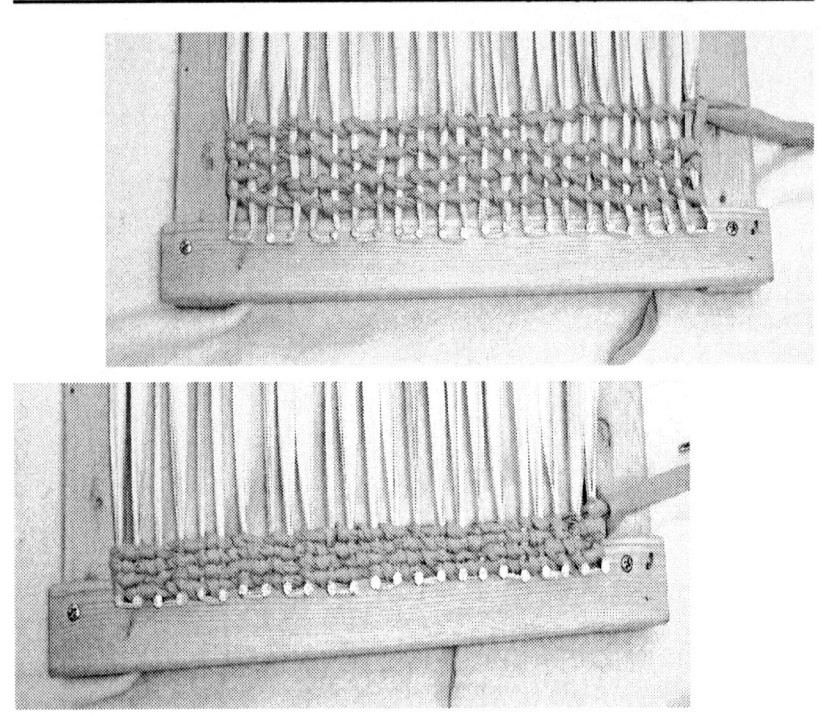

Basic needleweaving is usually worked back and forth in continuous rows. As more strip is needed for the weft on top of the frame, a new length is just threaded through several loops to secure it, just like in the darned rugs. Rows of needleweaving will slide readily along the warp, so you can work at a distance from the frame and then slide the completed rows into the desired position as shown above.

The appearance of basic needleweaving will vary depending on several factors. Using a heavier fabric (such a skirt-weight wool) will increase this technique's resemblance to traditional twining. Using very light fabrics (or yarns) will expose more of the warp if you want to do that.

Using the basic needleweaving technique, you can also vary the surface appearance depending on how the tension is held on the two weft strands. If both strands are under equal tension, the strips will twist around each other between the warp strands and give the impression of twining (as shown in the photos). If the underneath weft strand is held more tightly, the upper strand will wrap around it each time and have the appearance and structure of taaniko. (See Part II for more about the taaniko technique.)

Another way to vary the appearance of needlewoven rugs is to alternate the direction that the needle goes under the weft strand held under the frame.

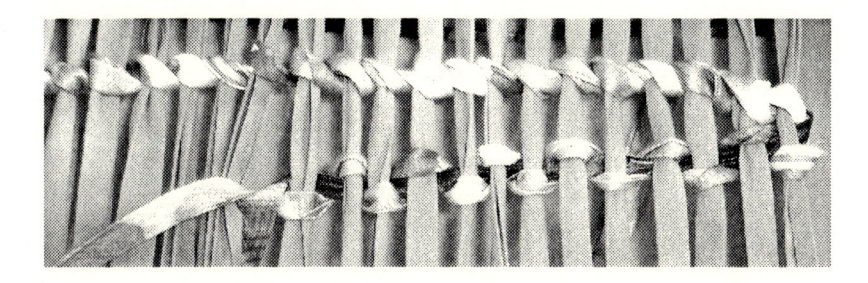

Notice in the top row of stitching shown, the needle is always inserted from the same side. If you alternate sides with each stitch instead, you can get a surface appearance which is of alternating loops. When rows of these alternating loops are pushed together, the rug appears to be a complex weave.

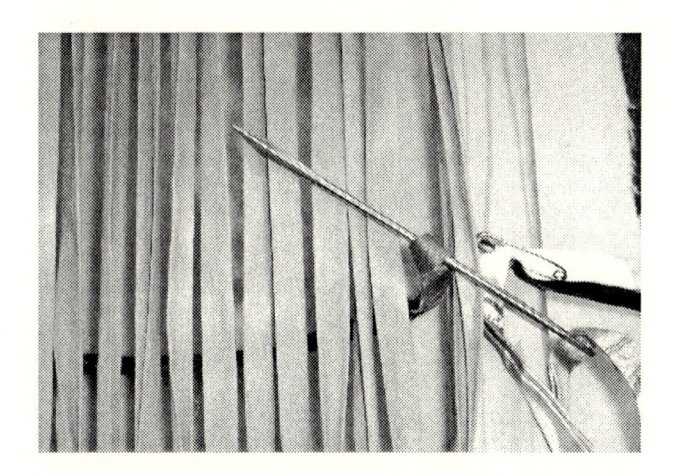

Finally, a Berber-like appearance can be created by another slight variation of basic needleweaving. For this texture, take the weft strand from underneath the frame, and twist it over the needle each time.

All three major variations can also be combined in a single rug to create textural designs.

CHAPTER 7
Locker Hooking

Locker hooking is a yarn rug technique that apparently developed in Great Britain and Australia in one form and in North America in slightly different form. In structure, locker hooking is part rug hooking, but unlike regular hooked rugs, the drawn loops are secured by a strand laced through them on the surface. Locker hooking is done with a special tool (a locker hook) which has a hooked end like a crochet hook with the eye of a needle at the other end. In North America, the same technique evolved using fabric strips, but the hooking was done with a regular rug hook and the loops were secured in a second step with a lacing needle worked under the drawn loops. In North America, this "anchored loop" technique commonly appeared on a burlap base, while in Australia and Britain, a special rug canvas was used with evenly spaced holes.

I've made many anchored loop/locker hooking rugs, some on burlap and some on rug canvas, but was never really satisfied with either base as a material for rag rugs. After fiddling with the technique on frames, I finally stumbled over the "obvious" way to adapt frames for locker hooking. Once having made a locker hooked rug on the frame, I'll not likely go back to the other bases, since locker hooking with fabrics just works so much better as a frame made rug. Also, the rugs made on frames have an all-fabric construction making them thicker, spongier and more durable.

There are two types of frames and warping that are ideally suited for locker hooked rugs: the pegged frame with ¼-inch warp spacing, and the scroll frame with continuous warping discussed in Chapter 22. If you are going to use 1½-inch cotton strip for the warp and the hooking, the pegged frame is great for small rug sections and the scroll frame if you want to make a larger rug in a single piece. If you want to use alternate materials that are significantly lighter or heavier for either the warp or the hooking, use the scroll frame.

A good locker hook for rug making has about a 1/8-inch diameter and is six inches long. The best hooks are steel. This is one of the few frame techniques where a special tool is needed. The same hook can be used to make rugs with yarns and roving as well.

If you made the square foot frame in Chapter 1, with nails or pegs at ½-inch spacing, you are ready to put the warp on for locker hooking. This warping is done in the same continuous fashion, but is wrapped around *every* nail (instead of pairs of nails or pegs) so that the warp is spaced at ¼" intervals (not ½"). If you have an **older frame** with pegs spaced an inch apart, the warping is done as a "suspended" continuous warp across the frame (see Chapter 20 for instructions).

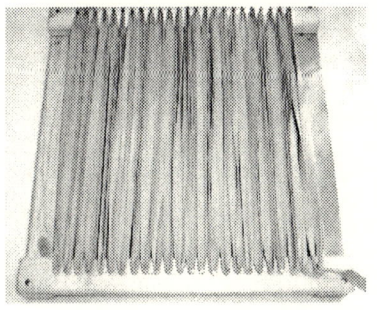

When your frame is warped, take a pair of small diameter dowels and place them across the warp strands, with one dowel above the warp and one below. Use rubber bands to secure the ends of the two dowels together. These dowels should be positioned four or five inches from where you intend to begin locker hooking. The dowels are needed to stabilize the warp strands until several rows have been hooked. They can then be slid forward along the warp if you are making a large rug. If you are using the square foot frame, the dowels can be removed when the locker hooking covers about a third of the area.

When locker hooking, you will be handling two different strips of fabric. One strip is held underneath the frame and will form the loops that show on the surface of the rug. This strip should be in one long, continuous strand and rolled into a ball for ease of use. The other strip of fabric is threaded through the eye of the locker hook. It is the anchoring strip and keeps the loops from pulling out. This strip is used in short sections—usually four or five feet. As you begin locker hooking, you can use strip from the ball to perform both functions. Once the anchoring strip runs out, you will need to change to a new section of fabric strip. The strip can be added, without sewing, following the directions below, or you can sew on additional strip using the bias joint for pre-folded strip or the overlapping bias joint for unfolded strip.

- To begin, pull four or five feet of strip off of the ball of strip. Bring the end underneath the frame and make an overhand knot with the strip to tie it to the first warp strand. Snug the knot down and thread the end of the strip into the locker hook.

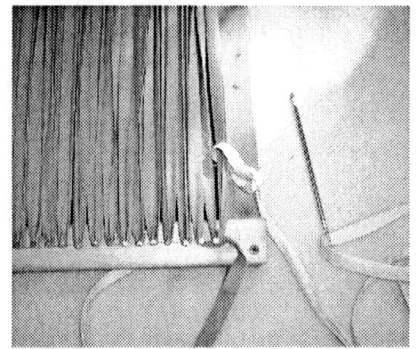

- Insert the hook between the first and second warp strands and pull up a loop of the strip from underneath the warp. The loop should not be tight to the hook—just a little loose to allow the anchoring strip to pull through.

Then pull up a loop between the next two warp strands, then the next two and then the next two so that you have four loops on the hook.

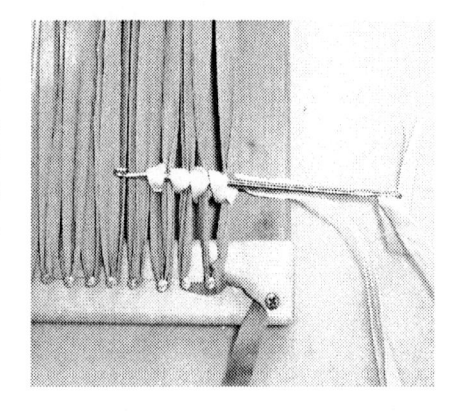

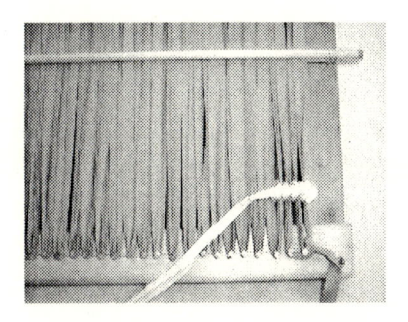

Locker Hooking

- Pull the locker hook through the loops and pull the anchoring strand all of the way through the loops as well. Arrange the loops evenly.

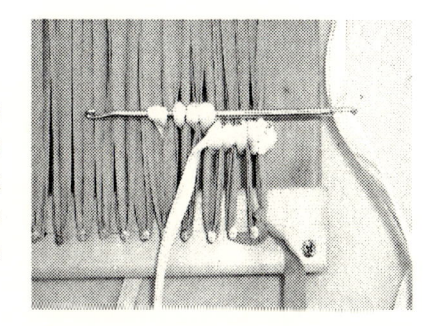

- Using the hook, pull up loops in the next four warp spaces and then pull the hook through the loops as well as the anchoring strip. If you are using unfolded strip, you may find that you need to twist the hook gently back and forth to ease it through the loops. If you are struggling to get the hook pulled through the loops, it generally means that the loops are being pulled too tightly.

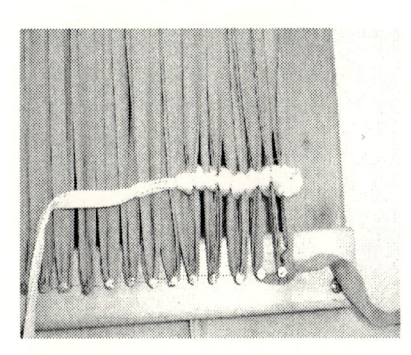

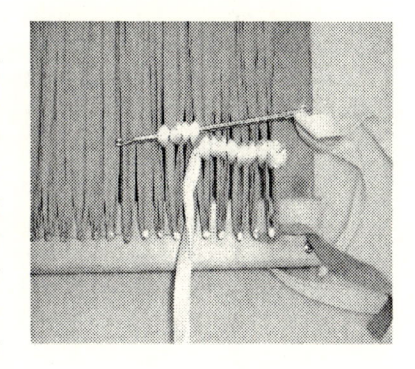

- Continue across the row pulling up four loops at a time and pulling the anchoring strip through the loops. Make sure as you work that the anchoring strip is not pulled so tightly that the warp strands are moved out of place. The last loop in the row is drawn up past the last warp strand.

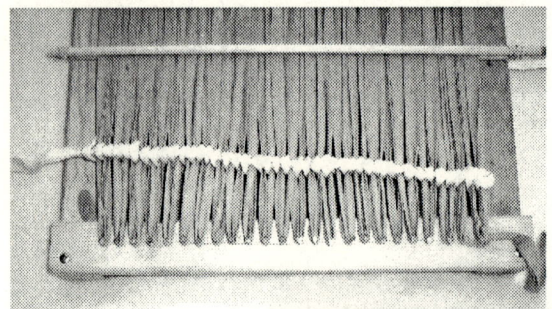

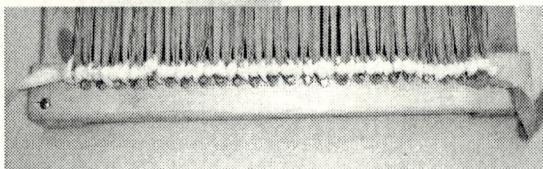

- For the second row, you will probably find it easiest to turn the frame around so that you can work back in the opposite direction. Begin by drawing up a loop between the first and second warp strands and add three more loops drawn from each of the next three warp spaces. Work across the row just as you did on the first row.
- When the anchoring strip is close to running out—about a foot or so from the end—you will want to plan where to have it end. The new anchoring strip can be added, without sewing, if the strip change occurs at least eight loops in from the edge of the warp. Look carefully at the length of the existing anchoring strip. If it will just make it to the end of the row, stop short so that the new anchoring strip will be used for the last eight loops.
- Cut a new section of anchoring strip about four or five feet long and thread the end into the locker hook. Insert the needle under at least the last five loops made and pull the new strip through, leaving just a small tail to show the end position. That little tail is needed to make sure that you don't pull the strip completely out of the existing loops.
- Continue locker hooking as before using the new anchoring strip. When you have completed the row and have made a few stitches in the next row, you can just clip off the tails left from the strip change. Clip off the tails from both the "old" strip and the "new" anchoring strip very close to the loops.

- When the rug surface is nearly complete, work a few rows next to the pegs at the far end, progressing along the warp to meet the already finished area. That procedure will make it so that the very last rows worked aren't right up next to the pegs, which is a difficult place to use the locker hook.
- To finish off the rug, clip the working strip and anchoring strip off at least six inches from the work, and bring the working strip up through the work. Then lace it under several loops. With the anchoring strip, work it back into an adjacent row of loops for several stitches. (Also, lace in any other tails from color changes that may still be loose on the back side of the work. Make sure to bring the strip over one warp strand before you bring it to the top. Then lace it underneath several loops.
- Remove the rug from the frame by gently lifting the warp strands off of the pegs. Lace the ends of the warp back into the rug.

The Fine Points of Locker Hooking

In the above instructions, you'll notice that I specifically mentioned making four loops at a time before pulling the anchoring strip through. I have found that four is the optimum number when working with fabrics. Beginners will often try to stack as many stitches on the hook as will fit and then find it really hard to force the anchoring strip through the loops. If you are working with a rough or coarse fabric, you may find that three loops at a time works more easily. Only if you are working with a really smooth fabric (or yarn) should you try working with more loops on the hook.

If you are working with very smooth fabrics, or if the rug is likely to see heavy wear and a lot of washing, you should sew the ends of the strips to the work. A few hand stitches is all that is necessary, since the sewing is only needed to keep the ends from working loose in washing.

When locker hooking, it is not necessary to pull the entire length of the anchoring strip through each set of loops. Pull through only the first foot or so and work to the end of the row. At the end of a row, pull on the anchoring strip to bring it all through the stitches. This procedure will allow you to use a longer anchoring strip (fewer strip changes) and saves a lot of time in pulling the entire strip through every set of stitches. The only caution in using this technique is that

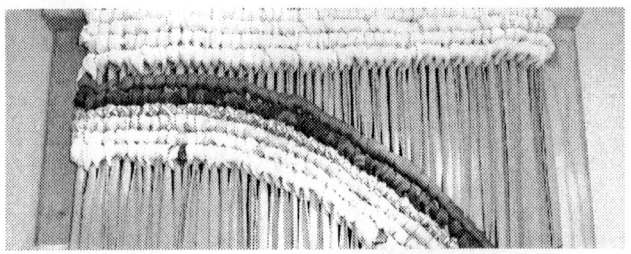

The front and back view of a locker hooking rug worked in sraight and curved lines.

you don't pull so hard on the anchoring strip that the warp strands are pulled in (waisting), so double-check each row before you begin the next to avoid that problem.

In locker hooking, it is the fabric strip held underneath the frame that forms the loops and the rug surface. When locker hooking is done properly little, if any, of the anchoring strip will show either on the front or back sides of the rug. Beginners will find it easiest to use the same fabric for the loops and the anchoring since that will disguise any unevenness in the stitches.

Beginners can most easily work in straight rows of locker hooking across the warp. Occasional color changes of the strip forming the loops will create stripes in the rug. That change can be done at any point by simply clipping off the "old" fabric strip at least six inches from the work and beginning with a "new" color, also leaving about a six inch tail. After another row or two of loops have been made, the two tails are threaded into the locker hook or a lacing needle, brought up to the front of the rug moving over one warp strand. The strip ends are laced under at least six loops on the top of the rug and then clipped off.

With a little experience working the locker hooking method in straight rows, you'll probably want to experiment with small areas of designs. You can begin and end locker hooking anywhere on the warp strands, filling in one area at a time. When you complete a small area, lace the ends back into the work. Bring both the working strip and the anchoring strip, over one warp strand and then under the loops on the front of the rug.

Just as with all of the other non-tensioning techniques in Part I, rows of locker hooking can be slid along the warp strands. However, with the ¼-inch warp spacing they do not slide as easily as methods using a wider warp spacing. For that reason it is important to make sure that each row is slid into position—fitting snugly up against previous rows—as soon as it is completed.

When you have a little practice with locker hooking, take a look at Chapter 8 with the advanced techniques. Locker hooking works well for patterns and designs in frame rugs.

An edge view of a locker hooked rug after it is removed from the pegged frame. Notice in this rug that a contrasting fabric was used for the warp. The warp loops show along the ends of the rug and are used to lace small sections into a larger rug.

CHAPTER 8:
Advanced Techniques with Non-Tensioning Methods

Making Large Rugs in a Single Section

If you've been working with the one square foot frame used in the previous chapters, there will come a time when you'll want to try making a larger rug in a single section. For the high/low pegged frame, there are a couple of things you should know before starting in on a larger rug.

First, note that the lines of stitching for all of the non-tensioning methods are worked across the warp strands in rows (more or less). For rectangular rugs, the most pleasing appearance is generally with lines running in the longest direction. If you want to make a rug where the lines of stitching run the length of the rug, the "high" sides of the frame have to be the two longest sides. That may look a little odd since most of us are still conditioned to thinking of frames in the same way that we think of looms, with the warp running in the longest direction, but remember that the frame is really a completely different tool.

The second thing to keep in mind with large rugs is the distance that you are able to reach comfortably. Almost all of the non-tensioning methods are done with one hand above the warp and one below. You don't want to make a rug five feet wide when you can't reach the center of it. However—and this is one of the most wonderful things about non-tensioning techniques—you can make a rug wider than you can reach, if you go about it in the right way. Take advantage of the fact that the rows of stitches can be slid along the warp threads. Work several rows of stitches within a comfortable distance of the edge of the frame. Then slide them into position in the *center* of the rug. Using that procedure, you gradually build the middle of the rug first. When the center is wide enough that the stitching is within easy reach, turn your attention to working from the edges toward the center.

Advanced Techniques with Non-tensioning Methods

Weaving Warp Strands Back into the Rug

With the all of the basic directions in Part I, the procedure for finishing the rugs is simply to lace the ends of the warp back into the rug, leaving the original knots in place. That is the surest way for a beginner to get a sturdy rug, since it is the warp strands that hold the rug together and if they loosen, so will the whole rug.

Once you have a little practice working with fabric warp strands, you can eliminate those corner knots for a neater appearance in the finished rug. You will need to plan ahead if you want to do this, and tie the initial knots holding the warp so that they have tails at least 12 inches long.

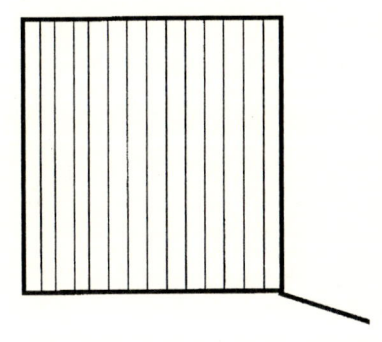

Have the rug completely finished, except for lacing in the warp tails, and remove it from the frame. Gently untie the knot from one corner, and thread the end of the tail through the eye of a lacing needle, tapestry needle or locker hook. Work with the back of the rug facing you so that you can identify the warp strands.

The tail should emerge from the very first warp strand on the side, so insert the needle along the path of the second warp strand toward the other end of the rug. Work the strand under several stitches (about three or four inches in) and then move over to the next warp strand's path and lace along it going back in the other directions for about two inches. Finally move over to the next warp strand's path and reverse the direction of the lacing again (working toward the opposite side again) and work the strand along that path for three or four inches again.

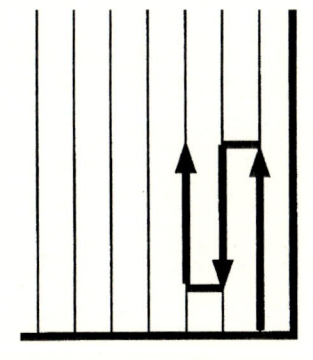

You can continue working back and forth until you run out of warp strand if you want to make very sure of anchoring the warp. The procedure of reversing directions as you lace the warp strand in will keep it from pulling out, but just to make certain, I suggest using a few handsewn stitches to hold it positively in place. The above directions are scaled for the one square foot frame, and for larger rugs you will want to extend the distance that the lacing is worked from four inches to about six. That is simply because there is more weight—and more tension on the warp strands—in a large rug.

When you've completed one corner, repeat the process at the other corner. This procedure of lacing in the warp strands is necessary to finish any freeform rug, so if you plan to make one, practice the technique on a smaller, square-cornered rug first.

Combining Non-Tensioning Techniques

All of the rug making methods in Part I can be used in the same rug to create a variety of surface textures. Any of the techniques using the ½" warping will work together without any adjustment, but if you want to add locker hooking to the mix, you will need to use the ¼" warping for the entire rug. The other techniques are then done using two warp strands at a time to maintain their correct spacing.

The biggest consideration in having combination rugs work is to keep the materials used for the rug surface of the same bulk of fabric (or fabric and yarns). They *do not* all have to be materials all of the same weight. For example, you can use heavy denim with light calico in the same rug if you adjust the width of the strips to have the same space-filling characteristics (bulk). Light fabrics will need to be cut wider than heavy fabrics. The way to test for bulkiness is to cut a test strip of the various fabrics and do a "twist test" with them. Each strip should be twisted into a cord. Then compare the diameters of the various cords and adjust the width of the strips until their diameters are approximately equal.

Inlays

An easy way to create a pattern or design in a rug is to do it in the fashion of inlays. The main body of the rug is completed on the frame, but the rows are not packed as solidly as you would if that was all there was to the rug. Once this background stitching is complete, slide rows together snugly to create an opening on the warp strands. These openings can be of just about any shape that the rows can be made to form.

Advanced Techniques with Non-tensioning Methods 67

This series of photos illustrates the process of inlay using a locker hooked rug. Above left, the background rows are worked, but not packed tightly. Above right, the rows are pushed together creating openings on the warp. Below left, a contrasting color is worked into an opening. Below right, the inlays are completed and the rug removed from the frame.

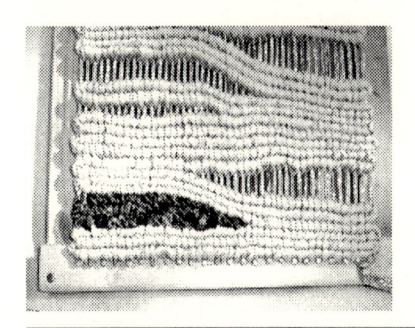

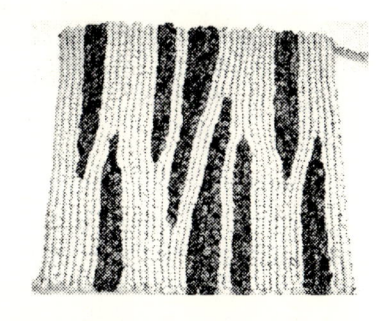

The photographs show an easy inlay made by sliding rows of locker hooking along the warp strands forming open wedges. The openings were then filled with more locker hooking using a different color of fabric (a plaid actually). Notice that the number of rows of inlaying is consistent across the width of the rug, keeping the same tightness in all of the rows. Do not do an inlay in one spot only leaving the other rows of stitching more loosely packed. If you design calls for a central contrasting inlay, that can be done, but you will need to add more inlays at the edges to keep the rows all tightly packed. For a central motif, these additional inlays can be done using the same material and stitching that was used for the background.

Free Standing Patterns

There are various ways to create a free standing pattern: do the pattern first and fill in the background; create the background first and then fill in the pattern; or create a foreground, middle ground and background. The photographs show rugs created each way, and I'll explain why each technique was selected for the particular rug.

The Padula Duck

Rug hookers have a term for made-up flowers in their rugs that don't really resemble any real flower. They call them "Padulas." Since this duck is of the same variety (with no resemblance to any duck I've ever seen), I thought he ought to be a Padula duck. The rug section is made entirely with the Amish knot stitching, worked back and forth.

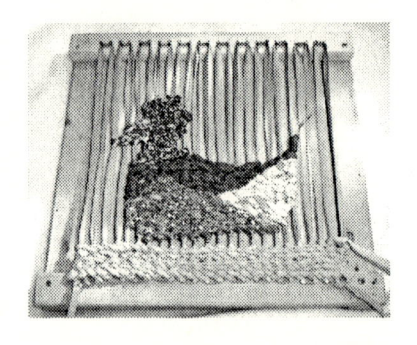

The toughest stitching to do on most any rug is the last bit since there just isn't much room to work, I find that it is usually easiest to work a central design first and then fill in the background. Typically, I will work a few rows along the pegs to keep the warp strands stable and then begin the central design. Especially if your design has curved lines, you'll find it helpful to follow the same procedure.

You can draw out your design on paper to use as a guide and then make just a rough sketch of the main areas directly on the warp strands. (Light colored warp strands make this easier.) Then fill in one area at a time. When two design elements touch each other and form a vertical line along a warp strand, you will need to lace one section into the next or a hole will form in the rug. (See the duck's chest where it meets the background for an example.)

If two design elements meet along a diagonal line or a curving

Advanced Techniques with Non-tensioning Methods **69**

The front and back of the completed "Padula Duck."

line that is mostly horizontal, you do not need to interlace the two sections. The duck's behind, where meets his back and belly, illustrates that type of relationship.

When the central design is complete, and the rows of stitching fit snugly together, you can finish filling in the background. Try to work the background so that the final rows are not near the pegs or right up next to the design area.

The Spider Mum

When the techniques that have a shaggy texture are combined with techniques that have a flat texture, you will find that it is easiest to work the shaggy part last. The long ends of the shags make it hard to see what you are doing otherwise. For the spider mum, the background of Bess Chet stitching was completely finished before filling in the flower petals.

The flower itself was done in circles working from the outside to the inside since the longest strands were at the outer edges. The very long strands are a sheer drapery fabric that would curl into a neat tube when pulled and the shorter strands are all T-shirt knits handled the same way.

The Calico Rainbow

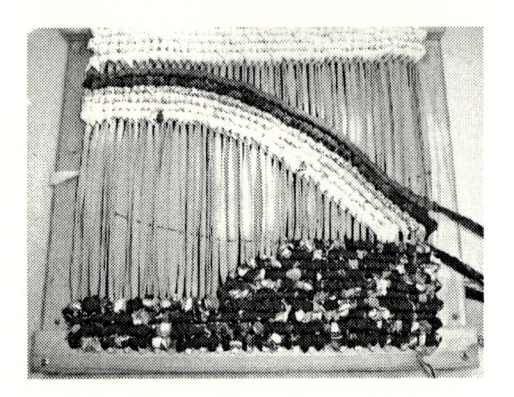

When you have a design that includes a foreground, middle ground and back ground, the design should generally be finished in that order. The rainbow rug is shown with the hills of the foreground worked first, followed by the rainbow. Then the hills which appear "behind" the rainbow are hooked, and finally the background (the sky) is added.

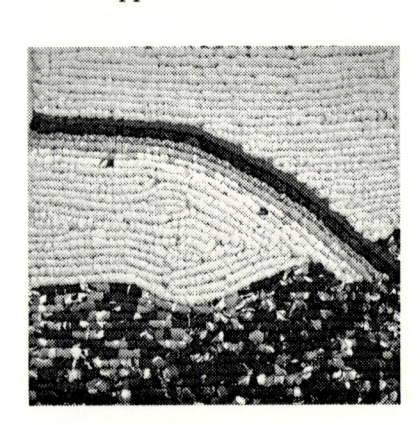

This example is done entirely with locker hooking which is the least cooperative of the non-tensioning methods as far as sliding along a warp easily. Because locker hooking has twice the number of warp strands as the other methods, it is best to work your design areas very close to their final placement on the rug.

Freeform Shaping

One of the most fascinating characteristics of working with a frame is that you can make rugs of nearly any shape on a square or rectangular frame. The technique requires that you use a continuous warp as shown for all of the rugs in Part I, and the warp itself must be of a smooth texture. A good quality broadcloth, cut into strips 1½ inches wide and double folded to bury the raw edges is the best choice. Do not use string or cotton "rug warp" for the freeform rugs, since they can break with the handling, and the rug will just fall apart.

If you just can't bring yourself to do the preparation work for the rug warp, the next best is the nylon cord sold in hardware stores

Advanced Techniques with Non-tensioning Methods 71

and sporting goods stores. It is smooth and has about the same bulk as the fabric strip. Don't use a macrame type cord that has ridges since it will catch on the stitching and make it hard to adjust.

If you are going to adapt this technique for yarns, the warp can be the smooth 6-ply linen which is sold for lacing together wool braided rugs. See the section on the use of alternate materials for more information.

There is only one really hard and fast rule when making freeform rugs with this method, and that is that no line which runs in the same general direction as the warp can curve toward the center of the rug. In the heart drawings, notice that the one on the left conforms to the rule, but the one on the right does not. Also, notice on the fish rug, that the end of his tail is straight up and down, not curved in to form two points, which would violate the rule.

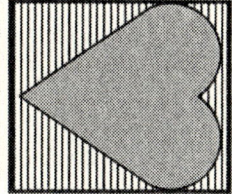

A good place to practice this shaping technique is to begin with an oval shape and then progress to more elaborate forms. The oval can contain designs or patterns. It does not need to be done with only a single fabric as the fish rug was (a brightly colored decorator print, by the way). Any of the non-tensioning techniques can be used to make free form rugs, but for your first rug, stick with the ones that use the ½" warping (not locker hooking).

- Use a high-low pegged frame with the pegs running on the longest sides of a rectangle.
- Wrap the pegs with a continuous warp at ½" spacing.
- With a marking pen, draw the outline of the rug (and any interior designs) directly onto the warp strands.
- With any of the non-tensioning methods, make two rows of stitches at the outer edges of the rug on each side. Do not work lines that run vertically along a warp strand though, such as at the ends of an oval.

Steps to create a freeform rug:

1. Outline the rug shape on the warp strands, and fill in the shape working toward the center of the rug.

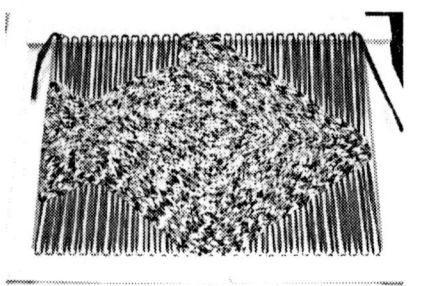

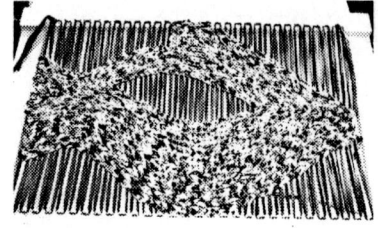

2. When the rug shape is completely filled in and the rows packed tightly together, begin removing the warp loops from the pegs. The warp loops are removed from the center of the rug first, on the top and bottom of the rug, working toward one end.

3. Remove one warp loop at a time, pulling through the slack in the warp.

4. When one end of the rug is completely free of the frame, start at the middle of the rug and work back to the other end.

5. After the rug is completely removed from the frame, check that the warp is snug all across the rug, and readjust it if necessary. Finally, clip the warp off a foot or more from the rug, and weave the ends back into the rug.

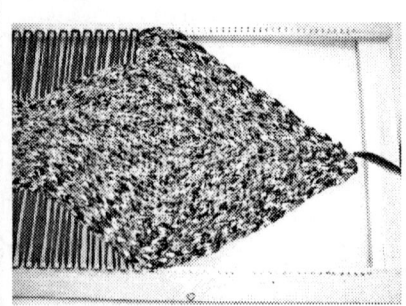

Advanced Techniques with Non-tensioning Methods

- Complete any design elements and the background, making sure that all rows fit snugly together.
- When the rug surface is completed, the rug is removed from the frame. Try to do this in one uninterrupted session because once the tension is released from the warp, the rows of stitching can spread.
- Begin at the center of the rug and remove two warp loops from the pegs on *each side*. (If your rug is an oval, continue removing warp loops, alternating the sides of the frame until you reach the point where the oval shape curves away from the pegs.)
- At the point where the rug shape does not fill the entire width of the frame (from one set of pegs to the other), you will begin pulling the excess warp through the rug. Hold the rug down with one hand, and pull on the warp strand so that it moves smoothly through the rows of stitches. This operation takes a steady hand—don't yank on the warp.
- Then on the opposite side of the frame, pull on the corresponding warp loop to take up all of the slack.
- Change to the warp loop on the other side of the frame and pull all of the slack in the warp through. The warp strands should come snugly to the edge of the rows of stitching but not buckle the rows and distort the shape of the rug.
- Continue working alternately on the sides of the frame working each warp loop in turn, and pulling all of the slack through. As you progress toward the end of the rug, you will be surprised at how much warp there is to pull through each time—but don't cut it off!
- When you reach the final row at the end of the rug, untie the original knot that secured the warp to the frame. When you have pulled all of the excess warp through, go back and check the rug shape. Adjust the warp if necessary.
- At the end, the excess warp strip can be cut to about a two-foot length. Thread the end into a lacing needle and, working on the back side of the rug, lace the warp back into the rug along another warp strand for at least four inches. Weave it back along a second warp strand going back in the opposite direction for about three inches. Then reverse directions again, and weave it along a third

warp strand for several inches. Then you can clip it off and sew the end in place with a few hand sewn stitches.
- Then start back at the middle of the rug and repeat the process for the other end of the rug.

Freeform rugs can be as wild as you want to make them as long as the design doesn't include any lines that curve toward the center of the warp strands. If you simple have to include a concave line, try re-orienting your shape to fit the rule. The warp strands can run the length of the rug if that is the only way to accommodate the desired shape, but for large rugs, it can be a real chore removing it from the frame.

In creating vertical lines along an edge of a freeform rug, note the placement of the vertical row. It must include the entire warp loop, not end between strands of a warp loop. The example fish rug has such a vertical line at the end of the fin on its back.

Freeform Shaping Applied to Three Dimensional Projects

I just knew that someone was going to ask the question about making baskets with these techniques, and felt obliged to include the basic techniques. Using the freeform shaping and non-tensioning rug methods, you can make baskets in two sections, or as a single piece.

For a basket made in two pieces, create the bottom of the basket in any shape appropriate for rugs with the freeform instructions given previously. Then using a second warping, make a section that is long enough to fit around the base. The two sections are then laced together to form the basket.

More interesting is the challenge of creating a basket (or vase or hat) in a single section. I've given two examples of possible shapes, but there is a lot of room for experimentation. The easiest for a beginner is the rectangular style basket, which is made in a cross shape. The piece is removed from the frame beginning at the center and working toward one end, just as in the rug directions above. The warp strands are tightened as each loop is removed from the frame. Once the cross shape is off the frame, the corners are folded up to meet and laced together.

Advanced Techniques with Non-tensioning Methods **75**

A round (or oval) basket is created without lacing—it is shaped by the tightening of the warp strands. The illustration shows one design for a basic basket. Note that—unlike rugs or rectangular baskets—the entire piece is removed from the frame before the warp strands are pulled tight. That requires a deft touch, so before you begin a round or oval basket, have a little practice with freeform shaping following the rug directions.

Shaping a Round Basket with Freeform Rug Technique:

1. Warp a square frame and outline the two halves of the basket as shown.

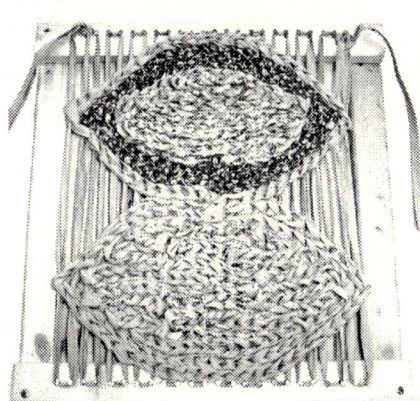

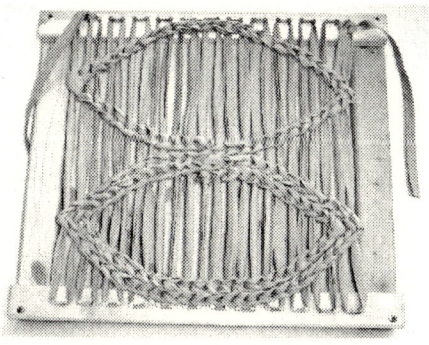

2. Fill in the sides of the basket, which can each have different designs.

3. Remove all of the warp loops from the frame.

4. Beginning at the center and working toward one end, pull the slack out of the warp strands. Work with one warp loop at a time, switching from top to bottom, just as in the freeform

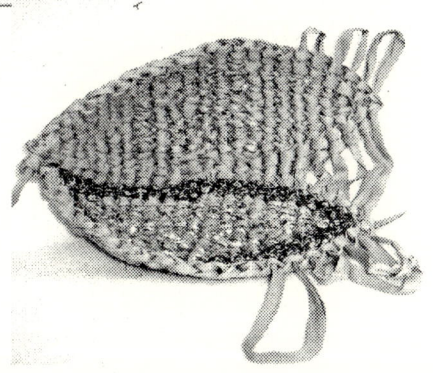

rug. Lightly hold the basket in shape as you pull the warp through.

5. Start again at the center and pull the slack out of the warp strands working toward the other end.

6. When all of the slack is out of the warp, shape the basket and adjust the warp as needed. Finish off the edge of the basket by using the excess warp to lace around the top edge with a whip stitch or other finishing stitch. Then lace the ends of the warp into the basket.

CHAPTER 9:
Non-tensioning Methods Worked Vertically

All of the rug making methods covered so far have been worked across the warp strands (horizontally). There are a few techniques that can be worked vertically as well. I really don't recommend these for beginners, since they all take adjustments by feel which can be frustrating for the inexperienced. Usually, these methods work best when incorporated in a design that has strong vertical elements.

The Flat Wrap

This technique has its origins in basketry and mat-making with natural fibers that are generally small and flexible (grasses, rushes, pine needles, bark fibers) so the flat wrap is very well suited to the use of fabric strip. The flat wrap is also a technique that will make a freestanding rag rug (not on a frame) and it is that technique that is modified here for use with warp strands. This modified flat wrap does not make as heavy a rug as the freestanding type.

- Begin with a ½-inch continuous or tied warp of 1½-inch folded fabric strip. Also use 1½-inch fabric strip for the stitches. Use a lacing needle or tapestry needle for the stitching. If you don't have one, attach a large safety pin to the end as a substitute for the needle.
- Cut a length of the working strip about five feet long to begin, and attach it to the first warp strand at a corner with an overhand knot. Leave at least six inches beyond the knot to work back into the rug later.
- To work the first row. Pass the lacing needle under the first two warp strands and bring it up to the top.

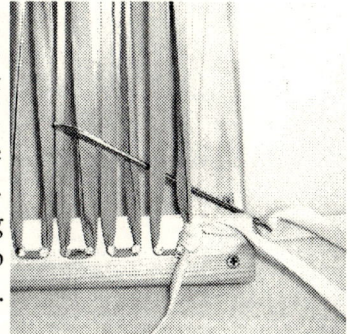

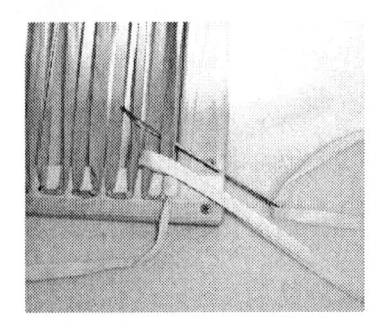

Pull it through snugly. Then, pass the lacing needle under the first warp strand only and bring it to the top. Pull it through.

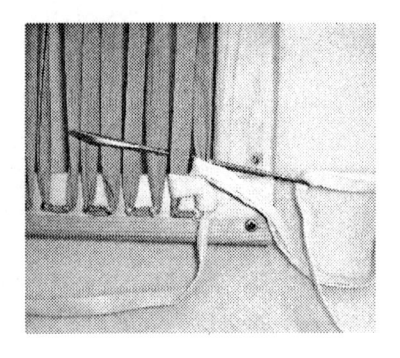

Repeat along the row, alternately passing the needle under two warp strands and then only the first. Try to keep your stitches spaced evenly and snugly together, but not so close that every stitch isn't visible.

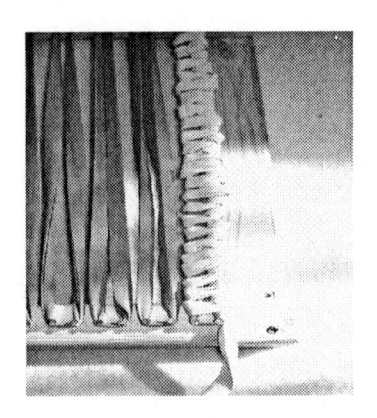

• When you have completed the first row of stitching, notice that between each "long" stitch a bit of the second warp strand is visible. It is in these spaces where the warp shows that the second row of stitching is worked.

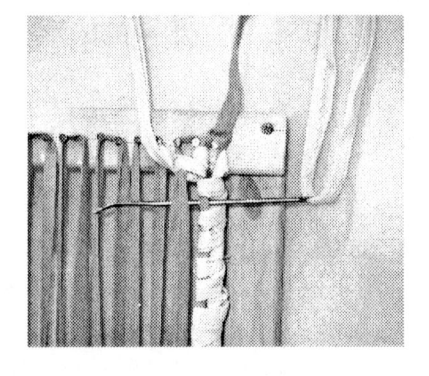

In this row every stitch goes under the second warp strand and up between the third and fourth strands. For those familiar with sewing, think of it as a large whip stitch. The flat wrap rugs can be done either using rows worked back and forth, or with all of the rows worked in the same direction (just start a new section of strip in each row.) Whichever way feels most natural to you is the one to use.

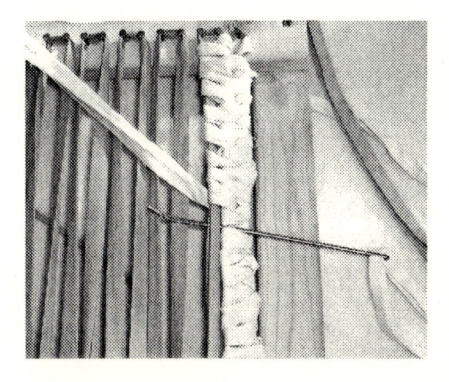

Non-tensioning Methods Worked Vertically

- For all of the rest of the rows, except for the very last one, the procedure is the same as the second row.
- When you reach the final row on the rug, the technique is very similar to the one for the first row. Between each full stitch, there is one wrap of the working strip around the last warp strand.

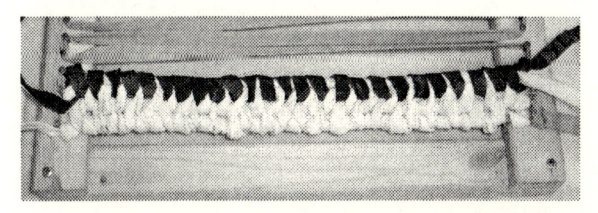

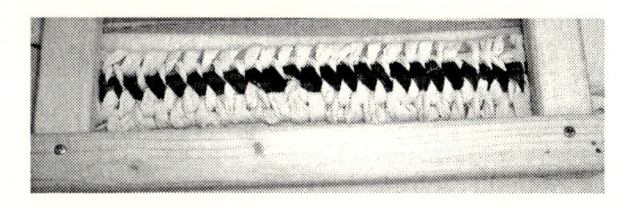

The texture of the flat wrap is accented by using contrasting fabrics. At left is the front side showing a dark row added to two light rows. At right is the back side showing two more light rows completed after the dark row. Note the basketweave effect that is created.

The Fine Points of the Flat Wrap

Whenever you run out of working strip, you can just drop the end, leaving at least six inches to work back into the rug later. Use the lacing needle and work the tails back up inside the stitches, running along a warp strand. The tails aren't a problem—actually they make the rug stronger. If the rug is going to see heavy wear and a lot of laundering, make a couple of handsewn stitches to keep the ends from working up to the surface.

This technique makes a medium weight rug, which is fully reversible. Take a look at the back of the rug as you are working though, since any pattern will show most plainly on that side. In the example shown, note that one row is done with a contrasting fabric to really show off the basketweave texture that this method creates.

For elaborate patterning, the flat wrap can be done with two, three, or four different colors worked together. The design is created by choosing which color you want for a particular stitch. Have all of the strips threaded with their own lacing needle. Stitch as usual with any of the fabrics, and hold all of the rest of the strips along the warp strand so that they get covered with each stitch. When you want to change color in your design, reverse the strip positions. Hold the strip that had been used for the stitching along the warp strand and pick up the new strand and begin stitching with it. If you've got a museum nearby, look at the ancient basketry for design ideas that you can work into a rug.

Figure-Eight Wrap

This technique is a cousin of the flat wrap and is completely compatible with it. In fact, most people will find it is easiest to make the first row using the flat wrap directions and then proceed with the figure-eight wrap. You can alternate between the two techniques in the same rug as is shown in the photograph. The figure-eight wrap makes a little more dense rug surface, but will not work with multiple strands the same way that the flat wrap does. Use it for background and texture variations.

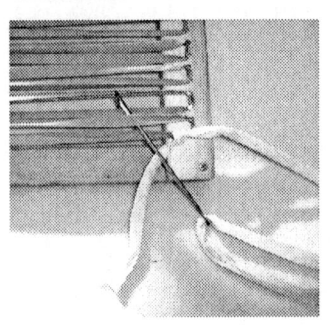

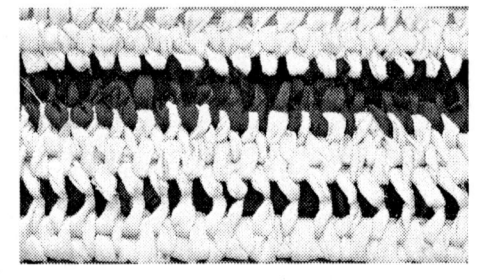

- The figure-eight wrap is made with a single strand of fabric strip, usually with a lacing needle, and is worked alternately around two warp strands.
- For the **first row** at the outer edge of the warp, make an overhand knot in the end of the working strip, securing it to a corner. Leave at least six inches beyond the knot to work in later.

- Using the lacing needle, work the strip underneath the second warp strand only and pull up the strip. Then insert the lacing needle between the first and second warp strands and pull it up outside the first warp strand. Repeat to make a loop over the first warp strand.
- Insert the needle under the second warp strand only. Then repeat going under the first warp strand twice to form a loop. Continue alternately working under the first and second warp strands in this same manner until the row is fairly well packed with stitches. You should just be able to see a little of the second warp strand between the stitches.
- For the **second row**, the strip will be worked in the plain figure-eight using the second and third warp strands. Place the stitches on the second warp strand between the stitches made in the first row. When that row is filled, make the next row in the same way over the third and fourth warp strands.
- Use the figure-eight stitching pattern for all of the following rows until you reach the last warp strand.
- In the **last row** at the other edge of the warp, a second wrap is added over the outermost warp strand only—just like the first row.

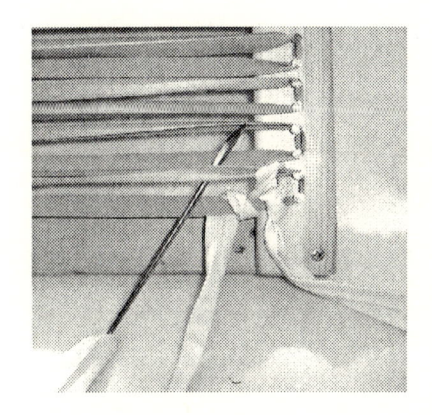

You can add an additional working strip at any point by dropping the end of the old strip, and beginning with the new strip at the same point. When the row is completed, lace in the tails from both strips underneath the wrapped stitches.

The figure-eight wrap can be worked back and forth in rows or you can begin a new strip for each row and work all of the rows in the same direction. Just like the flat wrap, the rug is reversible but the nicest appearance of this stitch will show on the back side of the frame.

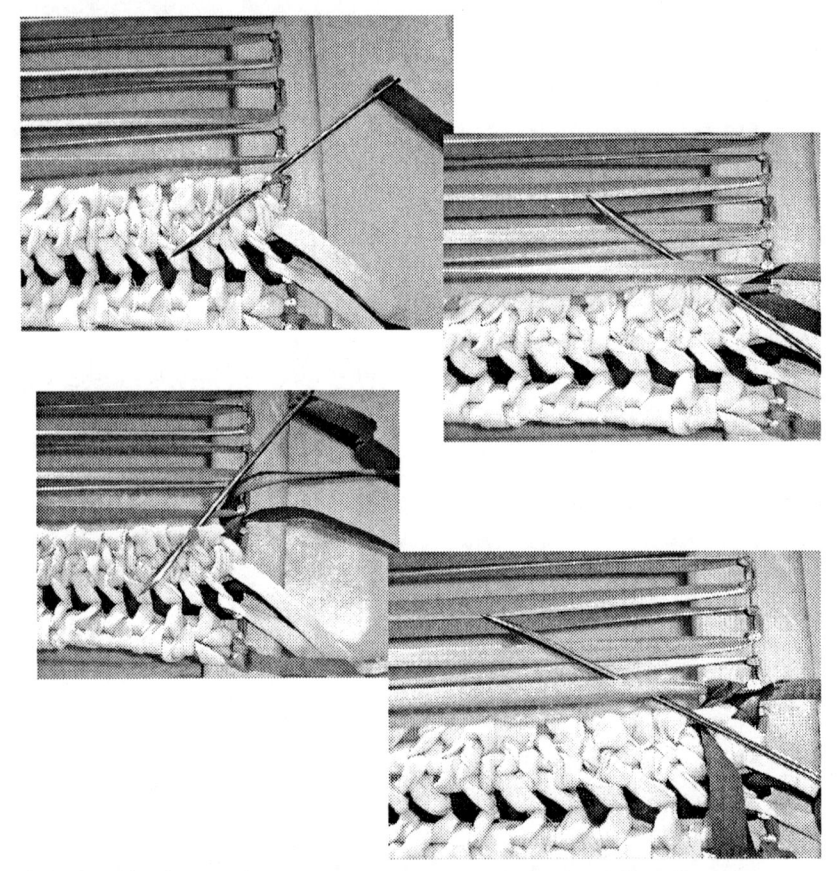

The photos above illustrate the beginning of a row working into an existing row. Note that the new stitches are placed between the loops of the previous row.

Two-Strand Figure-Eight Wrap

This method is a little more complex than the regular figure-eight wrap above, but it creates a very interesting patterning in the rug. Have a little practice with the regular figure-eight before attempting this. You can combine this two-strand method with the plain figure-eight wrap or with the flat wrap for interesting patterns and textures.

Work the two-strand technique with two different colors so that you can keep track of how the pattern develops. As you gain in experience with this technique, you can change colors of the strips as often as you wish to create even more elaborate effects. Color changes can be made similarly to the flat wrap by "carrying along" the unused strip color at the warp, or you can just drop and add strips and lace their tail ends in later.

I usually use two lacing needles with this method, but a safety pin on the ends of the strips also will work fine. For the first row along the edge, you should use a row of the regular figure-eight or the flat wrap, since the double-strand method is much harder to get an even stitch spacing with the extra loops around the outside warp.

The directions below begin with a row of this stitching done by itself in the middle of the warp strands. That will give you the feel of the stitch without having to interlace with another row as you are learning the wrap.

- Have your working strip double-folded for the neatest appearance. Cut a length of two working strips in different colors about five feet long. Use a large safety pin to secure the ends of the two strips between any pair of warp strands. For the sake of some clarity, I will refer to one strand as the light color and one strand as the dark color as are shown in the photographs.

- Bring the ends of both working strips to the outside of the pair of warp strands to be worked. (To correspond with the photographs, have the light colored strip on the right.)
- Bring the light strip over the right warp and under the left warp and pull it through to the left.

- Bring the dark strip over the left warp and under the right warp and pull it through to the right. It will cross over the light color.

- Bring the dark strip back, going over the right warp and under the left warp and pull it through to the left.

- Bring the light strip over the left warp and under the right warp and pull it through to the right.
- Then bring the light strip back over the right warp and under the left warp and pull it through to the left.
- This series continues with the strands worked alternately. Notice the pattern of small chevrons that are formed when the wrap is done in the correct sequence. If you notice a change in the pattern, that indicates there was a mistake in the wrapping at some point. Practice with the wrapping a little while, and then begin a row which will be interlaced with an adjacent row.
- While the two-strand figure-eight wrap can be done in a back and forth manner, while you are learning, begin all of your rows with new strip at the same end of the frame. The previous (completed) rows that you will be lacing into should be on the right side of the pair of warps that you will be wrapping.
- With one strip at the left side, bring it over the left warp then under the right warp. Use the lacing needle to bring the strip up around the right warp, between a pair of existing stitches on the right warp. Pull the strip up, then bring it under the left warp to the surface again. Repeat the same process with the other strip, and always bring the working strips back to the left side after each sequence.

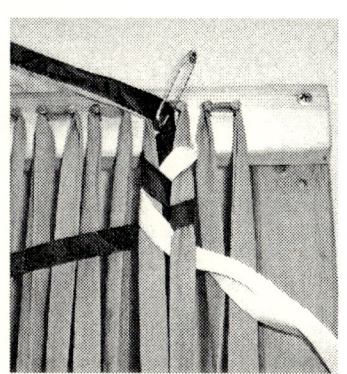

As you get a little practice with the method, you will notice that a pattern can be formed if you plan your wraps so that the little chevrons line up (a striped look) or with the chevrons offset (diagonal lines). Also experiment with one color sections separating the two-color sections.

When the rug is completely stitched, it is removed from the frame by pulling the warp loops off of the pegs. Lace the ends of the warp (and any ends left from the rows) back into the rug.

PART II: NON-TENSIONING METHODS USING A BI-DIRECTIONAL WARP

CHAPTER 10
Modified Soumak and Taaniko

A regular Soumak weave is a series of loops made across one set of warp strands. The modified Soumak is made in the same way except that each stitch is placed where the two layers of warp form a cross. For those familiar with hand sewing, it will be easiest to think of the process as a diagonal back stitch. The great advantage of working with a bi-directional warp with the Soumak is that each crossing of the warp creates a fixed position for each stitch. That allows for small areas to be stitched in a single color, akin to needlepoint done on canvas. This technique will allow for graphed patterns and you can use charted patterns for needlepoint, cross-stitch, etc., so long as they don't include too much detail.

A continuous warp is placed on the pegs from side to side as in the photo at left above. Then another continuous warp is wound

Creating the Frame and Bi-directional Warp

A bi-directional warp requires a frame with pegs on all four sides. You can use a flat frame with added pegs, or if you already have a high-low frame, you can add a board to the sides to create a flat surface as shown in the photo. The pegs should be evenly spaced on all four sides of the frame. They can be nails or screws on a 1/2-inch spacing or wooden dowels or pegs on a 1-inch spacing. The two matching sides should have the same number of pegs, but if you are using a rectangular frame, of course the longer sides will have more pegs than the shorter ends. The warp is done in two steps. The warping pattern in each step is the same continuous warp that was used for all of the rugs in Part I.

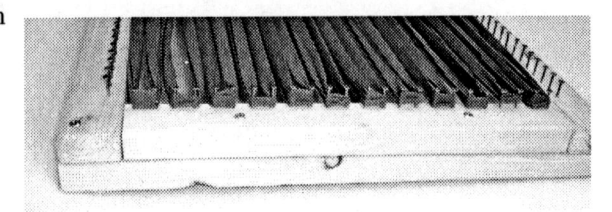

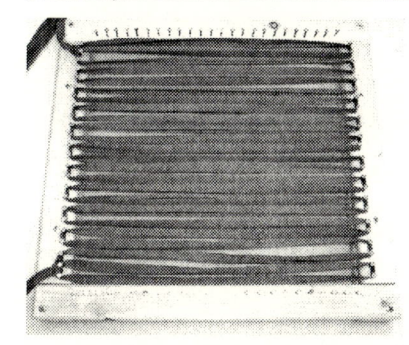

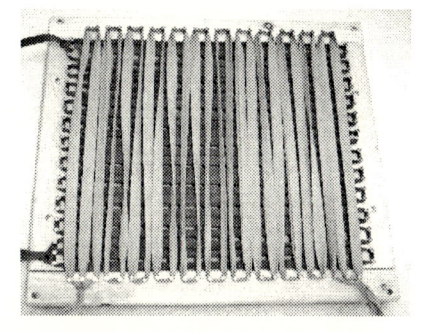

A continuous warp is placed on the pegs from side to side as in the photo at left above. Then another continuous warp is woun around the pegs at athe top and bottom as in the photo on the right. For illustrative purposes, the two warps are shown using different colors of fabric strip, but one color for both warps is generally more practical.

For the ½-inch warp spacing, use 1½-inch, double-folded cotton fabrics for both layers of the warp. The working strip is also 1½-inch double-folded cotton in the sample rug shown, but you can also use unfolded strip of the same width and weight, or one-inch strip from T-shirt knits. With lighter weight fabrics, the working strip will need to be cut wider or the rug will appear sparse. With heavier fabrics, you can either cut narrower strips and use them unfolded or use a less bulky material for warping (see the Handbook section for more information on alternate materials.)

Modified Soumak

Note that, unlike the rugs in Part I of the book, these stitches will not be able to slide around on the warp. These stitches will remain in their fixed position.

- Each stitch is worked under both layers of the warp, where the two strands intersect. Rows of stitches are worked in the same direction as the lower layer of the warp.
- Lace five or six feet of the working strip into a lacing or tapestry needle. Insert the needle at the corner of the frame, into the first loop of the upper warp and out at the first loop of the lower warp as shown.

- Insert the lacing needle between the second and third strands of the upper warp, bring it up so that it covers the first lower warp strand where it crosses the second strand of the upper warp.

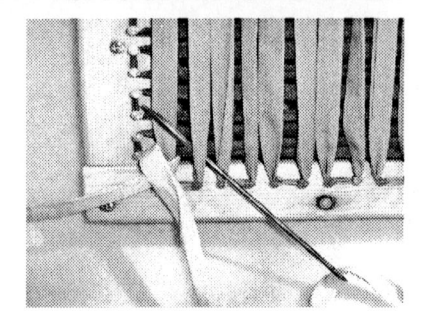

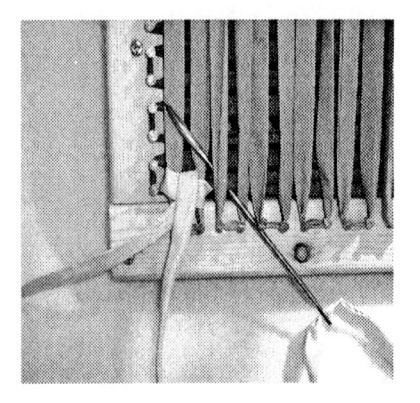

- Move to the space between the third and fourth strands of the upper warp and repeat the process to make the next stitch. For your first practice piece, continue across the row, following the first strand of the lower warp, making the same back stitch at each place where the upper and lower warps intersect.

- If you run out of working strip, lace the tail end of a new strip under several stitches and continue stitching using it. The tail end of the old strip will be laced under several of the new stitches.

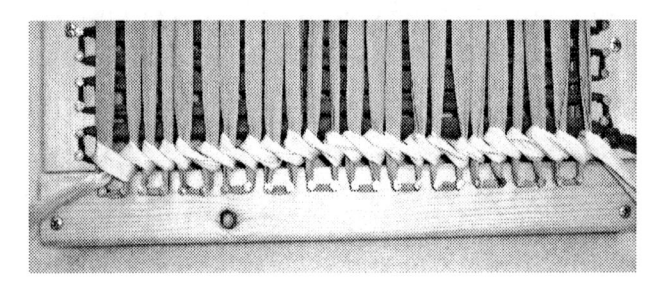

When your first row is completed, you have a choice. You can begin a new row from the same side with another section of strip. You can turn the frame over and work back in the opposite direction. Or you can decide you are ready to try out the fun part of this technique.

Modified Soumak and Taaniko

- With a section of strip on your needle, insert it under any warp intersection anywhere on the frame.
- Make three or four stitches going in the same direction as your practice row.
- Turn the frame over and make several stitches going back the other direction, then turn the frame over again and work back. You will have filled a small area with one color. Lace both ends of the strip underneath the stitches and clip them off.
- Change to another color of strip, and begin stitching next to the filled in area. Stitch short rows back and forth with it.
- If you want to change to a different location than where you are stitching, simply lace the working strip under several stitches until it comes out where you want it to be.
- Remember to work back and forth in rows (in the same direction as the lower warp), but you can work very short rows to have small areas filled.

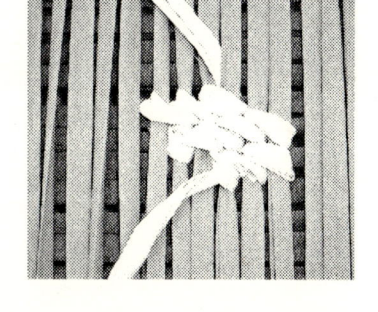

When you have worked a small area, check the back side of the frame. In solidly filled-in areas, you should be able to see a stitch at every warp intersection. (If you don't you can go back and fill it in.)

Keep the tension on your stitches fairly loose. They should fill the area without pulling on the warp strands in either layer.

If you are planning a stitched design, begin with one of the larger areas near the center of the rug and work in sections that touch it. Each section after the first should touch at least one other section to make sure that the design comes out and there are no gaps. In design work, keep the working strips fairly short (three feet or less).

Also, keep the tails laced into the work (don't let several accumulate). Try to keep the tails long enough so that they will be laced back in under at least six stitches and can't easily work out again. If you do end up with a particularly short tail (or if the rug will see heavy wear and a lot of laundering), hand sew a couple of stitches to hold the tails in place.

When your rug is completely stitched, it is time to remove it from the frame. Unlike the rugs in Part I, you will notice that there are loops of warp still visible around the edge. You have several options for finishing off those loops.

- You can remove the loops one at a time and make back stitches through them to form the edge.
- You can use a crochet hook to chain the warp loops together so that they lay flatter against the rug, or using more fabric strip, you can make chain stitches through each loop just like the Bess Chet method in Part I.
- You can also use fabric strip to weave across the loops in two rows of tabby (over one, under one) on all four sides.
- If you are making several small blocks of the modified Soumak, which will need to be laced together, just leave the loops alone until you are ready for lacing. When lacing, match and overlap the warp loops from two rugs, and use a back stitch through both layers of loops to join the rug sections.

Modified Taaniko

With the standard form of Taaniko, two working strands are used. One strand is held to the front of the work and is used to wrap around the warp and a second strand held behind the work. By using a bi-directional warp, you don't have to handle that second strand—the lower layer of the warp takes its place and simplifies the process. This modification of the Taaniko makes it very suitable as a beginning rug.

Follow the same directions for creating the bi-directional warp as above for the Soumak, using 1½-inch double folded cotton strip. For your first practice piece, also use the same type of strip for your working strand. If you notice that the rug is not quite as heavy as you would like, test a slightly wider working strip or you can a use a heavier fabric if you like.

Modified Soumak and Taaniko

- Install a bi-directional warp on the frame.
- Thread a lacing needle with about six feet of fabric strip.
- Insert the needle between the first and second strands of the upper warp, so that it passes underneath the first strand of the lower warp. Pull the strip through.

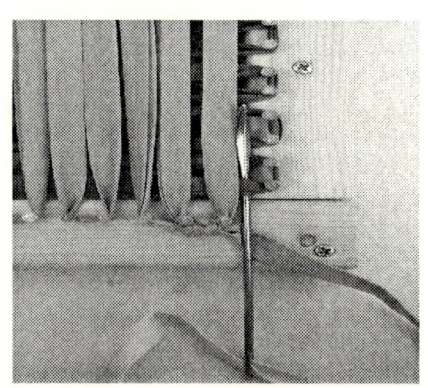

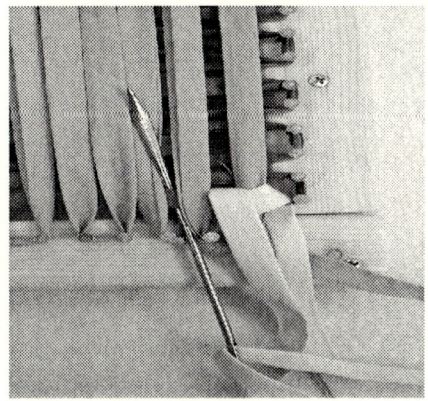

- Move over to the space between the second and third strands of the upper warp and pass the needle under the first strand of the lower warp. Pull the strip through.
- Repeat across the row making one stitch in each space of the upper warp.

- Lace in the tails at the beginning and ending of the row, or turn the frame over and work another row back in the opposite direction.

The really interesting feature of regular Taaniko is the way that patterns can be created. With this modified Taaniko, the same patterning can be done much more easily. In this modified technique two strands of different colors are used for the patterning, but they are both held above the warp. As you wrap with one, the other is laid along the top of the warp so that it is enclosed within the stitch. When you want to change the color of the stitching, simply reverse the strip positions. You can even use several strips of different colors carried along at the same time for really elaborate patterns.

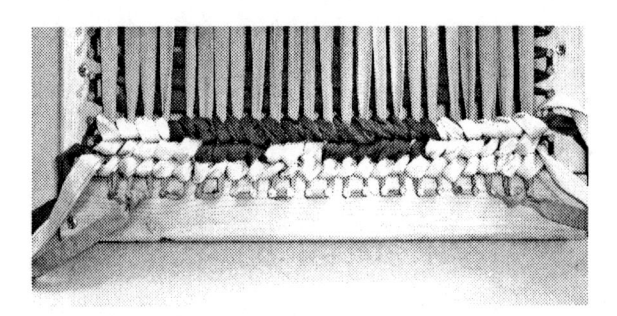

The more strips you add, the heavier the rug becomes, so stick to 1½-inch cotton fabric for all of the working strips (or other fabrics that have the same bulk). When changing from one working strip to the next, be sure to begin the wraps at the same space that the other strip last wrapped.

In the photo above, a simple pattern of Taaniko is begun using a dark and light fabric strip held on the top of the warp. When the light strip is used for the stitch, it shows on the surface because the stitch encloses the dark strip. When the dark strip is used for stitching, it is the one that shows on the surface. For your first pattern, begin by using only two strips held above the warp. Later on, you can use as many as you like. Keep in mind though that the more strips you use, the thicker the rug becomes. There is a significant difference between the thickness of rugs using two strands and those using four strands. If you don't want height/thickness variations in the rug, be sure to use the same number of strands throughout.

CHAPTER 11
Rya Knotting on a Bi-Directional Warp

Rya knot rugs have been made with yarns on a canvas base for a very long time, especially in Scandanavia, but they can be made with a rug frame and fabric strip as well with a minor modification. The basic rya is made with a needle. Each stitch forms a loop, which is clipped to form a shag piece. (Note: Do not use the unclipped loops for a floor rug. They are a tripping hazard and will catch bare toes, shoe heels, pet's feet, etc. Use unclipped loops only for wall hangings.)

The bi-directional warping used in the previous chapters also has to be modified a little for Rya knots. The first level of warp is the standard ½-inch continuous warp used previously. The upper layer of the warp is also a continuous warp, but each pair of warp strands is woven through the previous layer to give the base more stability.

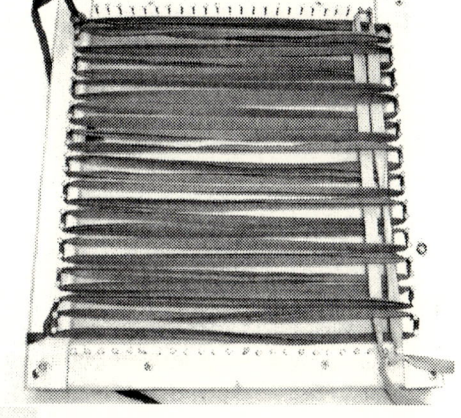

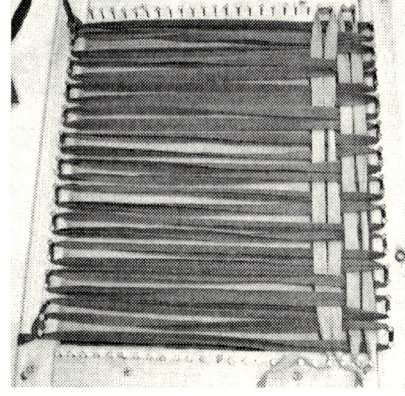

Use 1½-inch, double-folded cotton fabric for both layers of the warp. In weaving the upper layer through the lower layer, go over the first warp strand, then under the next *pair* of warp strands, over the next *pair* of warp strands and so on across. For the next weaving, begin by going under the first warp strand, then over the next pair, under the next pair, etc. Alternate for each set of upper warp strands as they are woven through the lower warp. When the warping is completed, the surface should feel firm, but not drum-head tight.

All sorts of different materials can be used for the Rya knots themselves. For beginners, I suggest using 1½-inch cotton material, torn into strips and not folded. This allows the knots a little more friction to keep from working loose. Double-folded strips will also work so long as the fabric itself isn't smooth or slick. (Of course, if you are making a wall hanging instead of a rug, anything goes.)

The working strip of fabric can be very short—even if it is only long enough to make one knot, that is fine. Just as in the Soumak in the previous chapter, the knots are made at the intersections of the warp strands. Use a large eye lacing needle threaded with fabric strip.

These rugs are most easily made beginning at the left side of the rya knot if you are right handed and from the right side of the knot if you are left handed. The directional cues in these instructions are for a rug begun at the left edge of the warp.

- Insert the lacing needle diagonally up, from right to left under any place where the warp strands intersect. Be sure to include only one warp strand from the lower layer and one warp strand from the upper layer in each knot. Bring the needle around to the top. Pull through the strip leaving a tail that is about the height that you want the shag to be.

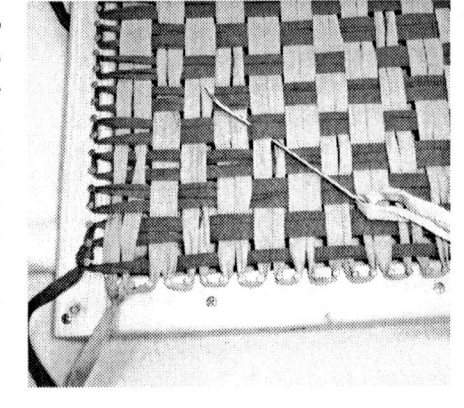

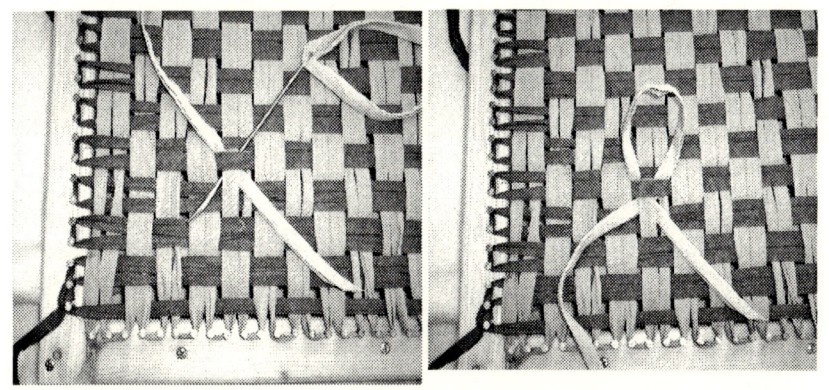

Rya Knotting on a Bi-Directional Warp

- Insert the needle diagonally down, from right to left, under the same warp intersection. Hold a loop of the height desired as you pull the strip through.

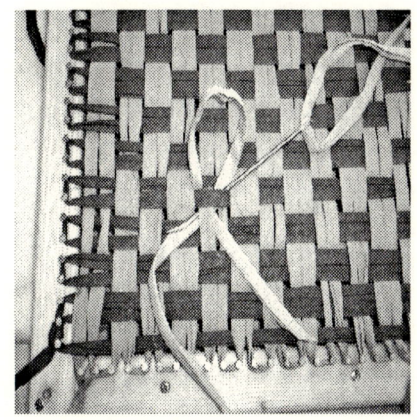

- Insert the needle diagonally down, from right to left under exactly the same warp intersection. (Yes, this is the same as the last stitch, but this time, don't hold a loop in the strip.)

- Pull the strip snug to complete the first stitch. Note that the very first stitch will always be somewhat looser than the following stitches made with the same strip.

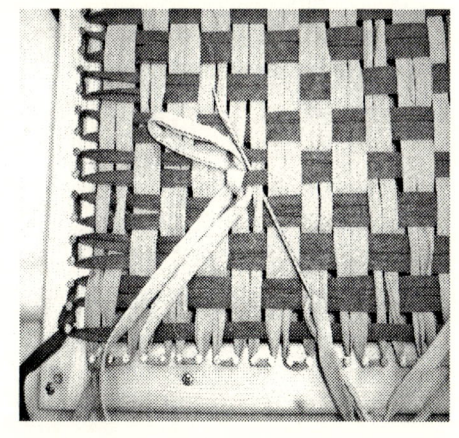

- To make your second Rya knot, you can move to any adjacent warp intersection.

- For the second, and all following stitches. Insert the needle diagonally and upward, from right to left under the warp intersection. Pull up the strip snugly.

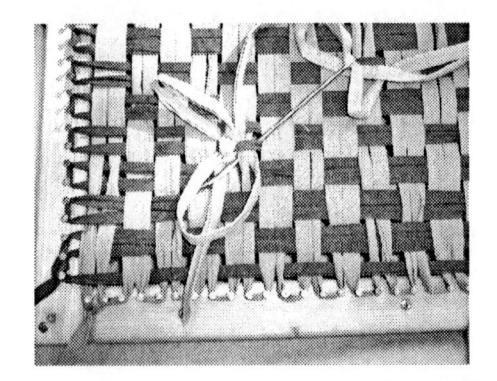

- Then, insert the needle diagonally and downward, from right to left under the same warp intersection. Hold a loop in the working strip of the desired height while you pull the strip through the stitch.

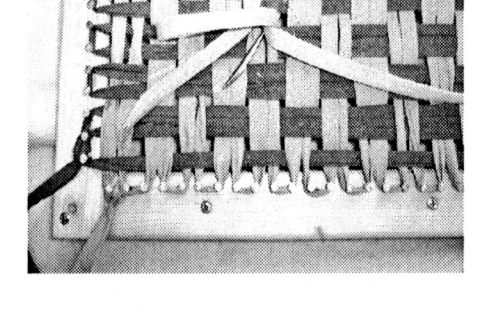

- Again, insert the needle diagonally and downward, from right to left under the very same warp intersection and this time pull the strip through snugly.
- Move to any adjacent warp intersection and repeat the process.
- Be sure to include the warp loops around the pegs in the knotting.
- When all of the knots are made, check on the backside of the frame to make sure that each warp intersection has a knot worked over it. Add knots to fill any open intersections. Then, on the front side, clip the loops to the desired height and remove the rug from the frame. Loops can be clipped as short as one inch if your knots are tight.

Rya Knotting on a Bi-Directional Warp

Rya knots modified for the bi-directional warp can be made in straight rows across, or back and forth in rows. However, this modified method is so flexible that you really aren't limited to working in rows at all. The technique is perfect for working designs into a rug, and because of the warping, the designs can be charted out on graph paper.

When working with a design, fill the center areas first and work toward the edges. You should make knots in the warp loops that pass around the pegs as well, but these can be a difficult space to maneuver in. One way to get around the problem is to knot into those loops using the knotted shag method and a crochet hook (see Chapter 2) or you can make a rya knot into each warp loop at the same time as you remove the rug from the frame.

Rya rugs really shouldn't be machine-washed because the knots can work loose with machine agitation. Shake them out regularly and vacuum them with suction only. For heavy soil, hand wash the rugs in a large sink or bathtub with lots of warm water, and rinse very well. Let them drain for an hour or so in the tub. Press out excess moisture with towels. Fluff up the shags and lay the rug flat to dry.

CHAPTER 12
Modified Hooked Rugs

This really is a wild-looking technique which, when completed doesn't really resemble a traditional hooked rug, but the method is virtually the same. I'd really suggest that these be made as chairpads, not rugs though.

Install a bi-directional warp on the frame following the directions in the previous chapter for Rya knotting. Use 1½-inch cotton fabrics for the warp.

For the hooked loops just about any fabric will do, but it must be bulky enough to completely fill each square in the warp. The structure of this rug depends on how tightly the warp is packed with loops. For the example rug, I used a roll of mill end fabric, four inches wide, of a loosely woven poly/cotton fabric. The mill ends are an inexpensive way to make these rugs since, with the height of the loops they can take upwards of four yards of 45-inch fabric per square foot.

- Use a very large crochet hook for the hooking.
- Begin anywhere that isn't right up next to the pegs—near the center is preferable.
- Have the hooking strip underneath the frame, and using the crochet hook, pull the end of the strip up to the top of the warp.

Modified Hooked Rugs

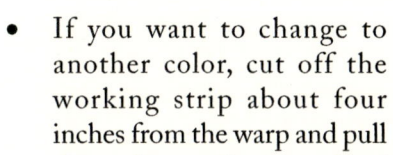

- Insert the hook in any adjacent space in the warp and pull up another loop.
- Move to the next adjacent warp and pull up another loop. Continue in the same way, pulling up a loop of fabric strip in each space of the warp. Do not leave any spaces in the warp unhooked. 
- If you want to change to another color, cut off the working strip about four inches from the warp and pull the end up to the front. Begin the next working strip as above.
- Work from the center of the rug outward, pulling up a loop in each space. The warp should be very tight by the time the hooking approaches the edges and you may not be able to hook loops through the outermost couple of spaces. That is actually a good thing because it demonstrates that the loops are packing the rug tightly.
- Remove the rug from the frame and clip the loops to the desired height. (If used as a chairpad or wall hanging, the loops can be left unclipped, or partially clipped.)

Using the Anchored Loop Technique for Rugs

The "anchored loop" technique developed in North America and is closely related to hooked rugs and to locker hooking used in Britain and Australia. Loops of the working strip are pulled up through the spaces in the warp, just like in the hooked rug above, but the loops are left low (about one inch). Then with a lacing needle or bodkin, a second strip is threaded through the loops to keep them from pulling out. For the surface of an anchored loop rug with the ½-inch bi-directional warp using cotton fabric or nylon cord, an ideal fabric is a lightweight wool cut about 1½-inches wide. The loops are hooked and anchored with the same strip and the resulting rug is thick and spongy.

Polar fleece can also be used for an anchored loop rug, and should be cut about ¾-inch wide. Cotton fabric or nylon cord is used for the warp.

PART III: WEAVING TECHNIQUES FOR USE WITH FRAMES

CHAPTER 13
Weaving on a Pegged Frame

Pegged frames can be used for weaving with a few modifications. In Parts I and II, the pegged frame is used with non-tensioning techniques. The warp strands did not tighten with each row worked, so once the continuous warp was in place, it did not have to be adjusted as the work got larger.

Weaving, however, does cause the warp strands to tighten, and so all of the weaving methods are considered "tensioning" techniques. As the weaving progresses, the warp strands will get stretched tighter and tighter, until it becomes impossible to continue weaving—or a weak warp strand breaks. To avoid that problem, there must be a way to release some of the tension on the warp strands, without having to restring the entire frame.

Different techniques of releasing warp tension can be used with each specific type of frame. The pegged frame, with pegs on all four sides, in this chapter makes an easy adjustment possible using only a dowel. If you have a pegged frame with pegs on only two ends, use the dowel as a "fifth stick" as discussed in Chapter 19.

Before beginning to weave on a frame, it is helpful to understand which types of weaving create the most tension on the warp. Each time a weft, or fill, strand crosses the warp, it tightens the warp a little, so the more often the crossings occur, the more quickly the warp will tighten.

- **Tabby.** This is the "plain" weaving that almost everyone has tried in one form or another with a school or craft project. The weft, or fill, strands are worked across the warp, going "over one, under one" all of the way across. The tabby weave is the one that will tighten the warp strands the most quickly.
- **Twill.** There are dozens of twill designs, but in all of them, the weft is worked over and under different numbers of warp strands. A couple of simple twill weaves would be "over two, under one" or "over three, under one" in working across the warp. The twill weaves will tighten the warp strands more slowly than a tabby weave.

There are so many good basic books about weaving, that I won't go into detailed directions about the weaving itself. Instead, the instructions are for using the various types of frames for weaving rugs. The most significant difference in working with frames, instead of looms, is that fabrics can be used both for the warp and the fill (weft) very easily, and the resulting woven rug is thicker and softer than rugs which use a string or thread warp. These all-fabric rugs are where a frame is by far the most practical tool.

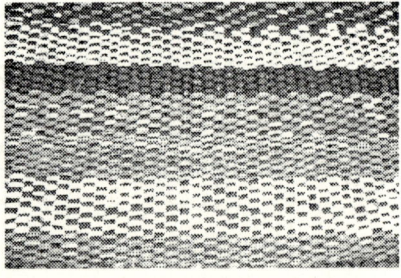

Above is the front and back sides of a simple twill weave (over 2, under 1) using a double-folded cotton fabric for the warp and the fill (weft) strands. Notice how the appearance of the two sides is quite different.

Using a Pegged Frame as a "Walking Frame"

The pegged frame, with a continuous warp, allows for rugs to be woven with four finished sides, two finished sides or with four fringed sides. I've often been asked over the years why there were pegs on all four sides of the old frames, and the answer is that very flexibility of rug design. When people think of rugs made on frames, it is always the woven rugs that are uppermost in their minds, but weaving on a frame quickly stymies the beginning experiment when the warp strands tighten too quickly.

The pegged frame that has pegs on all four sides can be rigged to accommodate tension adjustments for woven rugs, with just the use of a long dowel, rod or stout stick. The dowel needs to be long enough to reach between the pegs on the sides and about four inches more. The dowel must also be stout enough to hold the warp without bowing in.

For weaving a rug that is two feet wide, a ½-inch dowel is usually fine, but for wider weaving, a larger diameter will be needed. For very wide weaving, a piece of 1" X 1" lumber is fine, as long as there is enough room for it to fit between the pegs. On very wide weaves, the center of the dowel can also be tied to the frame to prevent bowing.

The example rug is made on a 2-foot by 3-foot pegged frame with the pegs set at one-inch centers. This was the most common size of the old pegged frames. The fabric used was a cotton blend with a spotty print, which disguises the weave.

Begin by installing a ½-inch continuous warp, just as for the non-tensioning methods in Part I. The warp should be of a cotton fabric 1½-inches wide and double folded for the neatest appearance.

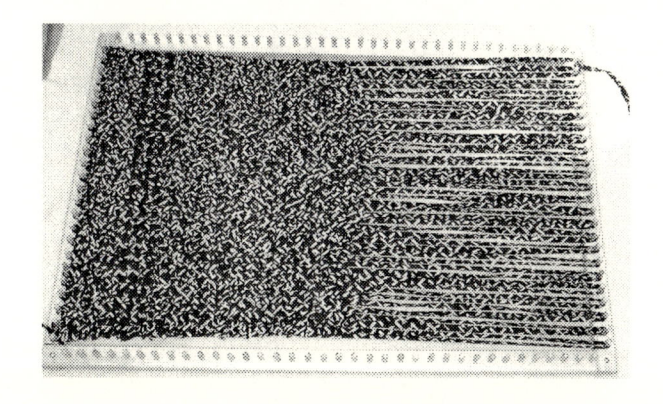

Unfolded fabric strip can also be used. For the weaving, select your fabric based on how heavy you want the rug to be. Light rugs are made using cotton fabrics cut or torn one inch wide. For a medium weight rug, cut cotton strips up to two inches wide. For heavy rugs, use cotton strips up to four inches wide or lightweight woolens cut up to two inches wide. Polar fleece and heavy woolens can be used up to a width of about two inches.

Start weaving at one end of the warp, leaving a short tail of strip to weave back into the rug on the second row. Weave away from the previous row in an arc to avoid "waisting"—do not weave a tight row straight across the warp. Use your fingers to pack each row of weaving tightly against the previous row. When the warp gets tight enough that it is becomes difficult to weave, the warp loops at the opposite end of the frame can be adjusted to ease the tension as follows.

- Hold the dowel between the end row of pegs and the first peg on the side of the frame.
- Pull the first warp loop off of the first peg and slide it onto the dowel.
- Move the dowel end forward to the second end peg, and pull the warp loop off of the peg, sliding it onto the dowel.
- Move the dowel forward again, and remove the third warp loop from the peg to the dowel. Continue across the entire warp, until all of the warp loops have been passed to the dowel.
- Set the ends of the dowel between the end row of pegs and the first peg on the side of the frame. Tie the dowel to the frame itself on both ends with a stout cord or fabric strip. Use a slip knot so that the knot can be easily untied if you need to move the dowel again.

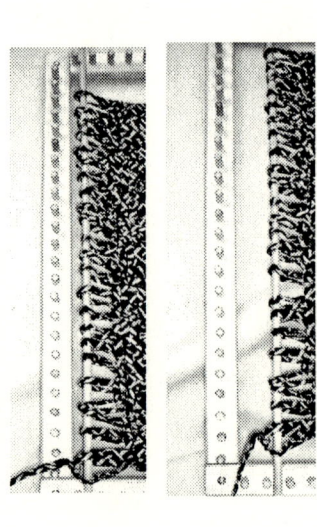

- You can now resume weaving, since some tension has been released from the warp.
- When the warp begins to tighten up again, just untie the ends of the dowel, move the dowel down to the next set of pair of side pegs, and tie it in place. Then resume weaving.

Depending on the type and weight of the fabric you are using for the weaving, you may need to adjust the warp tension more or less frequently. Generally, the heavier the fabric used for the weft, the more often the warp will need to have tension released. If you use double-folded cotton fabrics for both the warp and the weft, the weaving will be the flattest profile and the tension will not need to be adjusted very often. If you use denim, corduroy or wool for the weaving, tension adjustments will need to be made with every few inches of weaving.

Note that each time the warp strands have to be moved for a tension release, the length of the rug is decreased about an inch. For most rugs, that isn't a terrible problem, but if you want to buy yourself some extra room use the modified method below.

A "Walking Frame" Method for Longer Weaving on a Pegged Frame.
This technique is very similar to the "walking frame" above, but the warp is put on a little differently. You will need the same type and length of dowel that will fit across the frame.

- Before you begin to install a continuous warp, tie the dowel across the top of the frame between the third and fourth pegs at one end of the frame. This positioning is to allow enough room between the dowel and the frame to handle the warp strands. If you find that you need a little more room, the dowel can be moved further from the end of the frame.
- As you install the continuous warp, the end of the frame away from the dowel is handled as usual. At the end of the frame nearest the dowel, the warp will pass over the dowel, under and around the end of the frame, and then loop over the peg. Coming back, the warp follows the same path in reverse—going under the frame and over the dowel, back to the other end of the frame.
- When the frame is fully warped, begin weaving at the end farthest from the dowel.

- As the warp gets tightened up, and tension needs to be released, untie the dowel and remove it from the frame. You should be able to weave several more rows at that point, but may need to prop the far end of the frame up.
- When the tension again tightens, the next step is to move the warp loops from the pegs to the dowel. This is done a little differently than in the regular "walking frame."
- Hold the dowel outside of the pegs at the far end of the frame. Remove the first warp loop from the first peg, bring it back under the frame and around to the top. Pass the loop *between* the first and second pegs and onto the dowel.
- Move to the second warp loop and repeat the process. Then, repeat the process across, until all of the warp loops are on the dowel.
- Tie the dowel to the frame, outside of the end row of pegs.
- Then you can resume weaving. When the warp strands tighten again, the dowel is moved to the first of the side pegs, and tied in place.
- From that point on, the work proceeds just as with the regular "walking frame" above. When the weaving is complete (rows are woven right up to the pegs), the rug warp is ready to be removed from the pegs. This is done by removing one warp loop at a time and weaving through it. Have the weaving strip threaded into a lacing needle, and make sure that it is long enough to reach across the rug with about a foot to spare. As each warp loop is removed from the frame, pass the lacing needle through it. Pay particular attention to continuing the weaving pattern (if the rug is tabby). When all of the loops are removed from the frame, lace the end of the weaving strip back into the previous row of weaving for about a foot. Clip off the end and handsew the end in place to keep it from working loose.

"But What Do I Do with the Side Pegs?"

That is one of the questions that I get asked very often. Most people who try to weave on pegged frames, are so loom-oriented that it is difficult for them to think of weaving a rug sideways—but that is one of the beauties of a pegged frame.

If you install a continuous warp using the side pegs, it allows you to weave a rug with the lines of weft running the length of the rug, instead of across it. This has many advantages. First, since there are fewer lines of weaving, the problem of tension in the warp strands will be minimized. Second, with weaving the length of the rug, the weft strands can be shorter—each one only needs to be as long as the rug plus fringes at both ends—and fringes at the ends of the rug are where most people want them. (Of course, you can weave continuously, as above, for four finished sides if you prefer.) Finally, the weaver doesn't have to reach nearly as far across the frame to weave the width of the rug, as there just aren't as many rows to weave.

If you happen to own an old pegged frame with a stand, it is probable that the stand attaches to the ends of the frame. That is to make the use of the side pegs easiest for this type of rug.

- Install a continuous warp using only the side pegs of the frame.
- For fringes at both ends of the rug, cut the fabric strips for weaving about eight or ten inches longer than the frame. In weaving only one strand is used for each row.
- Weave each strand of fabric through the warp, leaving about four inches at the beginning and end that extend beyond the warp. Use your fingers to position each row of weaving solidly up against the previous row.
- If the warp tightens too much for comfortable weaving before you have woven across, use a dowel to create a "walking frame" as described above. However, in deciding whether to use a dowel or not, consider how much weaving is left to be completed. If it is only a row or two, don't use the dowel. Instead, just remove the warp from the pegs at the side of the rug where the weaving began. Weave the last couple of rows, and then you can remove the entire rug from the frame. If there is room on the warp to pack in just one more row of weaving, forget it, the warp and weft can be adjusted with your fingers to evenness, and call the weaving done.

- The end fringes will need to be hand-sewn in place so the end warp strands don't migrate and to make sure that the fringes lay flat. Don't do this with a sewing machine since the machine stitches will show. Instead use a good quality sewing thread and small back stitches. Working across the fringes, make a back stitch or two in each fringe and then two stitches which hold each fringe to the next one. The stitching line should be placed just outside the last warp strand.

Keep in mind that the rug structure really isn't stable until the fringes have been sewn in place, so don't remove the rug from the frame until you're ready to tackle the sewing. If you've woven a finished edge, the rug can be removed from the frame at any point.

Using Combinations of Techniques to Avoid Tension Problems

If you began your rug making with the non-tensioning methods in Part I, you're probably wondering why all the fuss about releasing the tension with weaving. "If the warp gets too tight, can't I just switch over to a non-tensioning method to finish the rug?"

The answer is yes, of course you can. But, weaving—especially tabby weaving—doesn't slide along the warp strands as easily as the non-tensioning methods do. So your rug would be mostly woven with some other stuff thrown in. That can make your rug look poorly made.

If you don't want to worry about making a "walking frame," but do want some weaving in your rug, some planning ahead is in order. When weaving on a pegged frame, the warp tension doesn't usually get to a critically tight tension until about half of the rug is woven (with tabby). That allows you to plan a combination rug with weaving and a non-tensioning technique so long as only half of the surface is done with weaving.

If you want a low profile, part-woven rug, choose one of the darned rug techniques as the combination. If you want a rug with various heights, combine weaving with a non-tensioning method that has a more raised texture, like the Amish Knot or the Bess Chet.

CHAPTER 14
Straight Weaving on a Flat Frame

Constructing and Preparing a Flat Frame for Weaving
  If you have a rug frame for hooking or a large quilting frame, you can use those for rug making. Stretcher frames for canvas are usually not stout enough by themselves for making rugs, but they can be used if the corners are braced. Most often, though, a person will have a particular size rug in mind and no frame to fit it, so a frame will need to be built. There are a couple of basic ways to build a flat frame—one in which all four sides are on the same level.
  The first and simplest option is to create a high-low frame (see Part I) and then add two boards on the sides to bring them up to the proper level (see Chapter 10 in Part II). That sort of frame is plenty strong for rug making, but in a large size will be heavy.
  The second option involves some basic woodworking skill. The ends of each of the four frame pieces are cut to half-thickness, so that when the pieces are joined, the corners overlap each other. Oddly enough, this is called a "lap joint." Frames made using a lap joint are strong, light and adaptable—especially when the corners are connected with a bolt and wing nut so that the frame can be easily taken apart and stored when not in use.

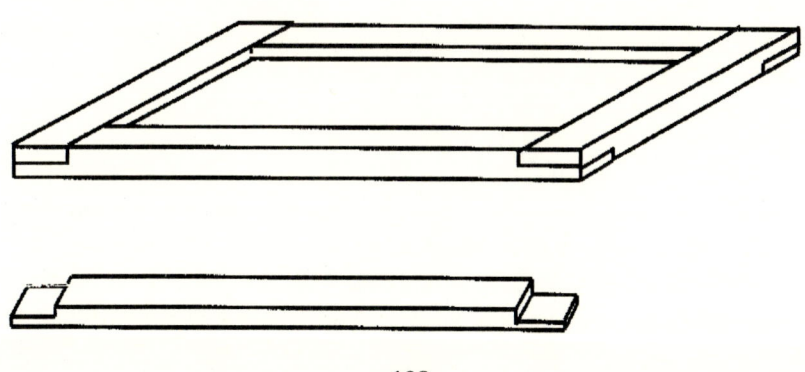

The most basic way to attach warp and/or fill strands to a flat frame is simply to tie them to the frame. This isn't a terribly efficient method since the warp strands tighten with weaving and the only way to release the tension is to untie and readjust every knot. At the right is a photo of a primitive flat frame with both the warp and fill strands tied to the frame. If you want to use tied on warp strands, see Chapter 19 for the "fifth stick" warping technique instead.

By far it is more efficient to use a frame wrapped with cloth strips so that each warp strand can be pinned to the frame for weaving. The frame is wrapped around with a double layer of cloth, so that T-pins can be used to hold the warp strands in place. As the warp strands tighten, the T-pins can be repositioned along the warp to release the tension. For the wrapping, select a fabric with a fairly low thread count (150) or less. You should be able to see the threads easily. The low thread count allows the T-pins to penetrate easily. Don't use heavy fabrics like denim or very light fabrics like cheesecloth. A medium weight, homespun type of fabric is the best for covering the frame.

Cut or tear the fabric into strips three or four inches wide. Begin wrapping at a corner opening, and wrap the strip around the frame in a spiral so that it overlaps on each wrap by about half the width of the strip. You can use a staple gun to hold the beginning of the wrap in place and to secure its end. Wrap all four sides of the frame twice.

Fabrics Used for Weaving on Flat Frames

The rugs in this chapter all look the showiest when the fabric strip for both the warp and the weft are prepared with a wide flat profile. Very heavy blanket woolens are cut about four inches wide and can be just folded in half. Coat woolens and heavy cotton fabrics, such as denim, can be cut 1½ -inches to three inches wide and double-folded. Lighter cotton fabrics are cut about six inches wide and can be rolled into tubes for weaving or triple-folded. The weaving will proceed most smoothly if the folds are pressed with an iron. (Heavy blanket wools don't iron well, so just fold them in half as you weave.)

Straight Weaving on a Flat Frame

This is the easiest type of weaving, and is begun in the center of the frame. Measure the frame on all sides and mark the center of each side. Using a large T-Pin, secure both ends of the center warp strand (the lengthwise strand) over the marks on the frame. Slide the T-pin into the warp strand sideways and into the wrapping fabric sideways as well. The pin should lay flat to the frame and the end of the pin should point to a corner of the frame. Don't use the T-pin like a thumbtack, since it won't hold. Also, to avoid multiple stab wounds, make sure that the end of the pin doesn't point toward the top or bottom edge of the frame.

Because the weaving proceeds alternately in the horizontal and vertical dimensions, there isn't a true "warp" or "weft" with these rugs. For the sake of clarity in the directions, I'll be referring to the strands worked in the longest dimension as the "warp" and the strands worked in the shortest, or horizontal, direction as the weft.

- When the first center warp strand is pinned in place, secure the first horizontal (weft) strand in the center of the frame. These rugs are made with weaving at the same time as the strands are added so the rug builds from the center.
- Add the next two vertical warp strands, one on each side of the center strand. Pin them in place. They should pass over the center horizontal strand.
- Add the next two horizontal strands, one on each side of the

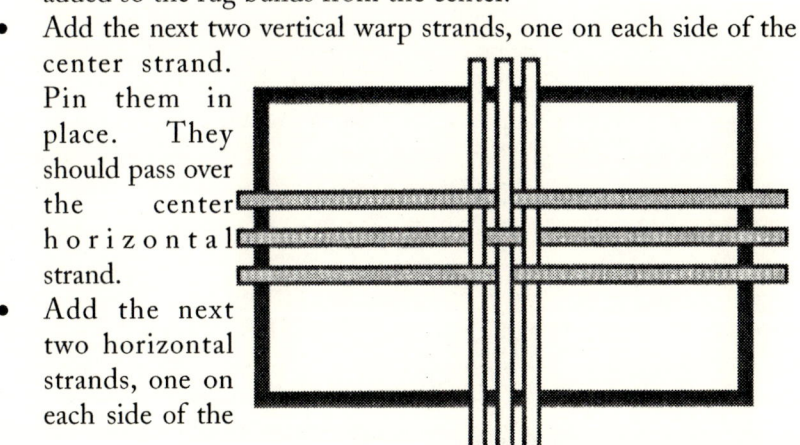

center strands. Notice that these strands will have to be woven through the three vertical strands at the center.
- Add two more vertical warp strands, one on each side of the existing strands. Weave them through the horizontal strands and pin the ends in place.
- Add the next two horizontal strands, weaving them through the vertical strands, and pin their ends.
- At this point there should be sufficient friction in the woven section that you can adjust the weaving with your hands so that it is straight and tight. The most recently woven strand at the outside will not stay in position yet, so don't try to fight with it. Instead, as you progress with your weaving, position the strip that just preceded the current weaving.
- Continue across the rug, alternately adding and weaving the vertical and horizontal strands in pairs.
- If your rug is rectangular (not square), all of the vertical strands will be in place before all of the horizontal strands. At that point, just continue weaving the horizontal strands.
- When you notice that the strands in one, or both, directions are getting too tight to weave easily, it is time to reposition the pins. Work with one strand at a time, and only on one side at a time. Remove the T-pin from the strand, let the strand relax and reset the T-pin to hold it. (Hint: If your T-pins start pulling out of the wrapping, it is time to reposition the strands!)

When your rug is completely woven, it is time to remove it from the frame. The edges will need to be hand sewn, so have a needle and thread handy. Decide whether you want four fringed sides, fringes only on the ends with finished sides, or four finished sides. You can also make a bound edge. Just follow the appropriate set of directions below. Before you begin removing the rug from the frame, do a final adjustment to the weaving with your fingers so that it is as even and neat as possible.

For a fringed end or side, begin at the first strand in a corner. The ends of the strands that stick out are sewn directly to the edge of the last woven strand. Use small back stitches that just penetrate to the other side of both the vertical and horizontal strands. Sew across, unpinning one strand at a time, just as it is ready to be sewn. When one side is complete, do the opposite side next. When all four sides are sewn, pick up the rug and gently(!) shake it from each of the four sides. That helps the weaving "settle in." Lay the rug flat for trimming the fringed ends if you want to. Use a yardstick and chalk line to get a good straight cut.

For a finished end or side, begin at the first strand in a corner. Remove the T-pin from that strand only. Each strand will be brought around the last strand of weaving, and its end tucked under the next strand, where it is hand sewn in place. This means that alternate strands will be brought to the top of the frame (where it is easy to sew) and then the next strand will go to the back side of the frame (where it is next to impossible to get at). For that reason, the strands are removed one at a time and then pinned in their proper position—either to the front or the back of the first weaving strand. Remove the strands from one side, then the opposite side, then the two ends. Handle the rug carefully since it will be full of pins at this point. Then, working on a table, begin sewing, working along one complete side. Take the pin out of the first strand, and cut it to length so that its end will be hidden under the second weaving strand. Sew through all three layers making sure to secure the cut end. Use small stitches to hide the sewing. Trim and sew each strand along one side, then do the same for each side in turn until they are all secured. When the sewing is completed, gently shake the rug from all four sides to settle the weaving.

For a bound edge, you can use a sewing machine. A bound edge looks the nicest when it is made from the same materials as the rug. Cut strips for the binding four inches wide. For heavy fabrics, the binding strips can be cut on the bias. Light fabrics really aren't suited for rug binding since they wear through too quickly, but if that isn't a concern, cut them on the straight grain. Working across one end of the frame, remove the T-pin holding each strip, then use it to pin the strip to the first weaving strand that it crosses. If you don't like handling all of the pins, baste the strips to the weaving strand instead (which is a lot safer). When the rug is completely off of the frame, trim the ends of the strips on all four sides so that they extend just about one inch beyond the last woven strand. Lay the rug binding, face down on the rug aligning the edge with the trimmed ends. Sew across with a one-inch seam allowance. You are aiming to get the sewing line right at the edge of the last woven strip. Sew the binding to all four sides. Tuck the rug binding to the back of the rug, and take a look at it. If there are bulges where it folds over, trim the offending strip back a little shorter. Turn the rug over, and fold the rug binding to cover the ends of the trimmed strips. Turn under a hem on the rug binding so that its edge aligns with the edge of the last woven strip. Pin the binding in place and miter the corners neatly. The binding can then be hand sewn (best) or machine sewn (if you're very careful).

Making a rug longer than your frame is possible, but requires some careful handling. Prepare the strips for the length of the rug—not the length of the frame. All of the lengthwise strips are then pinned to the frame. The excess strip in each warp strand is carefully rolled up and secured with a rubber band. (The extra length of strip should all be on the same end of the frame.) Weave the strands across the warp, beginning at the other end, not at the center as above. Position each weaving strand with your fingers so that it fits snugly against the previous strand. Note that these strands do not need to be pinned to the frame.

When the warp strands begin to tighten up, you can loosen the tension by repositioning their T-pins. When there is only about six inches of space left on the frame, baste around the two sides and the beginning edge to stabilize the position of all of the strands. Carefully unpin the basted edge and the warp strands. Reposition the rug on the frame, pinning the woven section to the frame at one end and the individual warp strands at the other end. Then you can continue weaving. Finishing is the same as for rugs made the same size as the frame.

"Straight Weaving" can also be done on the diagonal, using a frame. The weaving is exactly the same tabby weave and the rug is begun at the center. The only difference is that the weaving strands are set diagonally on the frame. Secure the ends of each strand with T-pins. The diagonal weave looks a little fancier, and is an easy way to get the look of a frame braid, without quite as much work. The edges can be finished with the same techniques as the regular straight weaving (fringed, finished or bound). If you plan carefully, you can also trim these diagonal rugs to an oval shape.

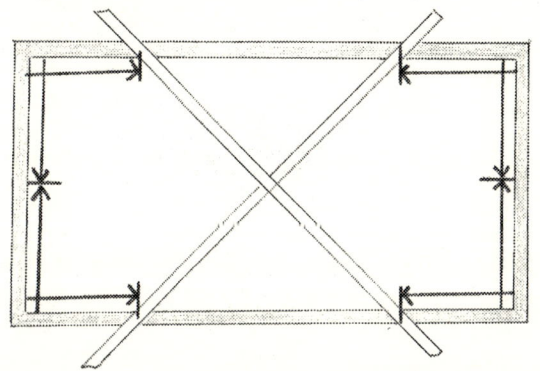

For an oval rug, begin the weaving at the center of a rectangular frame. The first strands are placed away from the ends of the frame by one-half of the width of the frame. Then the weaving proceeds as usual, adding strands to alternate sides of the center strands. When the weaving is completed, remove the rug from the frame and trim it to an oval shape. A bound edge is the most practical for oval rugs.

To make a rectangular rug with a diagonal weave, place the first strands at the corners of the frame and weave outward from them. This makes a very showy rug when the edges are trimmed straight and the fringed ends are hand sewn in place.

There are many other variations of basic weaving that are adapted to the flat frame. A simple variation is using two different colors, one for the warp and one for the fill strands in a simple twill weave. This creates a bi-color rug with one color predominating on each side of the rug.

Above is shown the front and back sides of the same rug using this simple method. The warp was of the dark fabric and the light fabric was woven through using an over-two, under-one twill.

Another easy, but showy variation for frame woven rugs is made using a plain tabby weave. The warp strands are added with two strands of light colored fabric alternating with two strands of dark colored fabric. The weft (fill) strands are also alternating pairs of light and dark colored fabric. Note that this weave works best with fabric strips with a flat profile.

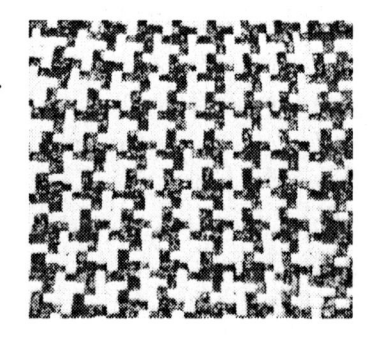

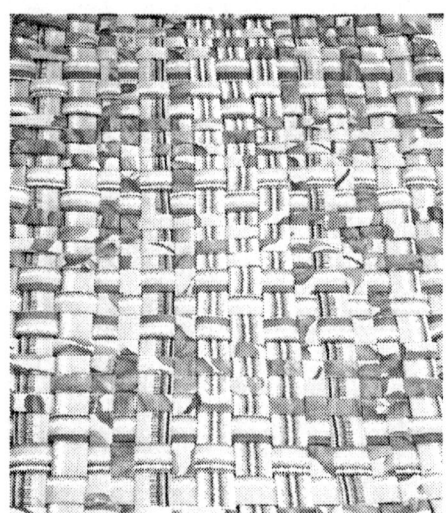

Of course, there are unlimited variations possible by selecting different fabric types and prints for the weaving. At left is an example of a striped fabric combined with a large print fabric in a rug. The two fabrics were also prepared at different widths to create a visual complexity that isn't possible with solid colors.

Weaving on a Flat Frame

For the adventurous rug maker, the most interesting variations occur by mixing yarn and fabric in the warp and the weft on a flat frame. These combinations present an entirely new field for design for the experienced weaver with effects that can't be achieved on a loom. The example on this page is made of double-folded, lightweight wool strands in light and dark colors combined with a linen cord for both the warp and weft. The linen can be pinned to the wrapped frame by winding it around a T-pin in a figure-eight. The fabric strands are pinned as usual.

To achieve the pattern below, the warp sequence is: 1 dark wool, 1 light wool, 1dark wool, 1 light wool, 1 dark wool, 2 light wool, 1 dark wool, 1 light wool, 1 dark wool, 1 light wool, 1 dark wool. Then the sequence is reapeated.

For the weaving, the weft sequence is: 1 dark wool, 1 linen, 1 dark wool, 1 linen, 1 dark wool, 1 light wool, 1 linen, 1 light wool, 1 linen, 1 light wool. Then the sequence is repeated.

Note that in the photograph, the warp strands are shown in a horizontal position and the weft strands are shown running vertically. This is only one example of this type of frame weaving and many other effects await the rug maker's creativity.

CHAPTER 15
Frame Braids

Ok, so technically these are "plaits," not braids, but that is the most common term for this type of rug. Think of these frame braids as straight weaving set on the diagonal. There really isn't a "warp" or "weft" since each strand is used the same, so I'll just use the term "strands." One nice thing about the frame braids made on a wrapped flat frame, is that you don't have to have a frame as large as the finished rug. Each section of complete braiding is stable enough to baste at the edges, and then the whole business can be moved along the frame to do more weaving.

One problem that seems to come up for people is figuring out how long to make the strands for a frame braided rug of a particular length. It looks like it ought to be a complicated math problem, but it isn't. Just add the length and width of the rug that you desire, and that's how long the strands will need to be. For example, for a rug two feet wide and three feet long, cut the strands five feet long. For a rug three feet wide and five feet long, each strand will need to be eight feet long. Add a little extra allowance if you're not sure about the length of fringes that you want, or if you are planning a complex pattern. If you aren't using strands that have a flat profile, you will want to add about 20% to the calculated length.

To determine how many strands to prepare, you will need to know the width of the individual strands and the width of the frame. You will need twice as many strands as will fit across the frame. For example, if your frame is 24 inches wide, and your strands are one inch wide, 24 strands will fit across the top of the frame. You will need twice that number (48) strands to make the frame braid.

With the frame braids, you'll be much more confident (and do a better job) if you have made a rug with straight weaving in the previous section. The same tabby weave is used for the frame braids and the same type of fabric strip, so the straight weaving is a good way to learn the basics before taking on the less-intuitive frame braids.

The trick with frame braiding is that the strands are added, woven and secured in opposing pairs. One strand of the pair will go to the right diagonal and the other strand will go to the left diagonal. Fabrics for frame braids can be of a heavy cotton or light wool (cut four inches wide and double-folded), light cottons (cut six inches wide and triple-folded) or heavy wool (cut two inches wide and folded in half).

- Begin by marking the center of the top of the frame. Measure how far the center mark is from the corner. Make a mark on each side of the frame that is the same distance from the corner as the center mark. These are the only guides you'll need.
- Select two of the prepared strands to be the first pair. Pin them at the center mark with a T-pin, so that one strand points to the left, diagonally, and one points to the right, diagonally. Leave three or four inches of each strand above the pin for a fringe at the end.
- Where the strips cross the guide mark on its own side of the frame, use a T-pin to secure it in place. Let the strip ends lay outside the frame.

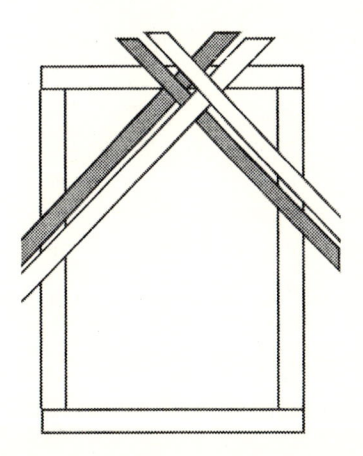

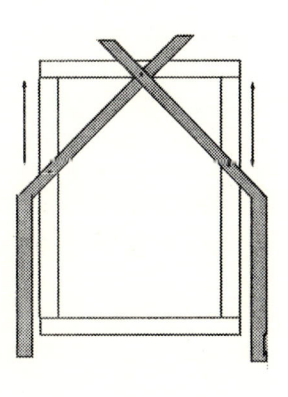

- The second pair of warp strands is placed on the right side of the center pair, so that the strands just touch. One strand will go down to the right and one strand will go down to the left. Look closely at the illustration, though. The strand which points toward the center pair will be pinned below the guide mark on that side of the frame, and the strand which points away from the center will be pinned above the guide mark on its side of the frame. Also, note that the strand pointing toward the center pair will actually begins the weaving sequence as it passes over the strand from the center pair.

- Add the next pair of strands immediately to the left of the center pair. The strand pointing away from the center of the frame will attach to the side above the previous strands. The strand pointing toward the center of the frame will attach below the previous strands.
- Note that these strands are woven through the existing strands when they cross them.
- Add the next pair of strands to the right of the existing strands following the same procedure. The following pair of strands is added to the left side of the existing strands. Keep adding pairs of strands, on alternate sides until the top of the frame is full. Weave each added strand where it crosses the previously attached strands.
- When the top of the frame is filled, you should have a central section of weaving also completed. From this point, the strands are woven from alternate sides, beginning with the strand at the top of the rug.
- Each strand is folded at the edge of the frame and re-pinned so that it is pointed toward the center of the frame. Then weave the strand through the existing strands, and pin it just below the last woven strand on the side of the frame.
- Adjust each row of weaving with your fingers as you weave, and every so often, go back and readjust all of the woven strands so that they lay evenly and on a true diagonal.

Frame Braids 121

Above is a detail of the edge of a frame braid rug in progress showing the T-pins securing each braid turning along the side.

- If your braid begins to outgrow your frame's length, baste the top edge and the sides where the weaving strands were folded back. (Look carefully at the photograph above, left. It shows a frame braid rug, a little more than half completed, but there is no room left on the frame for more braiding. It is ready to be moved along the frame.) After basting, unpin the rug from the frame, move it up and re-pin it in the new position. The basted sections will only need pins about every three or four inches. Be careful when re-pinning the weaving strips to the frame to make sure that they are in the correct order.
- When the frame braid is completed, baste across the bottom edge and remove the rug from the frame. At the right is shown a frame braid rug just after removal from the frame and before the end fringes have been trimmed. The pattern in the rug developed because

the central five pairs of strands were of a dark color, and the remaining pairs of strands were all of a light color.
- Frame braids can have fringed ends or bound ends. (See the previous chapter on how to use those finishes.) You can also do a finished end by folding the strips back and working them into the rug, but the number of strands usually makes this type of finish too bulky.

If you want to begin your frame braid with a finished edge, you will need to prepare your strips for weaving twice as long.

For example, if your rug is two feet wide and three feet long, normally your strips would be a little more than five feet long. To begin with a finished edge, strips for that rug would need to be cut ten feet long.

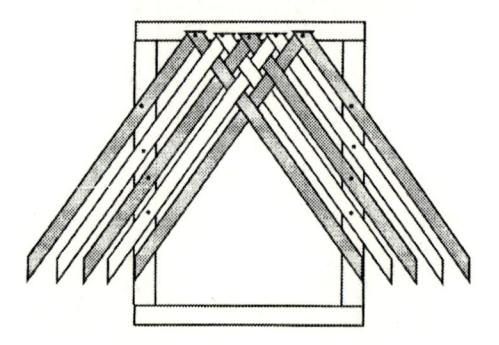

The strips are folded on the diagonal as they are first attached to the frame (see illustration) and then the frame braid is completed as above.

CHAPTER 16
Wagon Wheel Rugs in Round and Oval Shapes

These rugs are very showy, and not nearly as complicated to make as they look. The unique character of these rugs is in how the warp is handled, being added as the rug progresses. Because these rugs require weaving around a curve with wide strips, some practice is needed to make sure that the weaving strand is not pulled so tightly as to form a cup in the rug.

The name "wagon wheel rugs" seems to have been derived by the use of old wagon and/or carriage wheels for the rug frame. Round (or oval) frames are not required to make these rugs, however, which is good because those frame shapes can be hard to find in appropriate sizes for rugs. Instead, a square or rectangular flat frame can be made in any desired size. The frames for wagon wheel rugs are wrapped with cloth (see Chapter 14 for the directions for building and wrapping a flat frame). As with the straight weaving and the frame braids, the strands of fabric forming the spokes of the wheel are attached to the frame using T-pins.

The same types of fabrics are used for wagon wheel rugs as in the previous two chapters, but because the weaving is curved and has to be eased, skill is required to properly just the tension of the weaving and the placement of the strands—especially for fabric strips with a flat profile. I've found that people will have a lot less trouble with a wagon wheel rug, if they have first made a rug on a flat frame using the straight weaving.

The very first wagon wheel rug that I ever saw was one of Swedish origin, made entirely of wool, which had been pre-folded to create neat tubes. These wool rugs take a little longer to make, but really are the epitome of wagon wheel rugs. If you decide to make one, see the Handbook section for instructions on pre-folding wool strips.

Once your frame is ready and the weaving strips are cut you are ready to begin the rug. Select four of the weaving strips which are at least 6 inches longer than the diameter of the frame. Pin them to the frame with T-pins so that the strips are firmly stretched on the frame. (Hint: If you are working with children you can baste the strips to the frame so there are no pins or tacks to poke small fingers.) These four warp strips should be held to the frame tightly enough that they don't sag to the tabletop underneath, but should not be stretched to a twanging tightness.

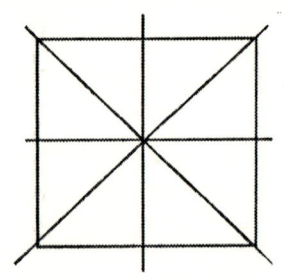

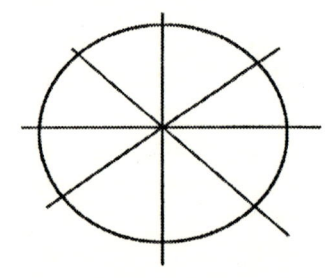

- Place the strips as shown for the shape of the frame you are using. The four strips must all cross at the very center. Sew through the center several times making sure to attach all four strips.
- The weaving of a Wagon Wheel rug is a standard over-and-under (tabby) weave. But in order for this type of weaving to work you have to have an *odd number* of the radiating strips to weave around the circle. Therefore, the weaving begins by laying a strip next to any one of the original "spokes" to make that odd number for weaving.

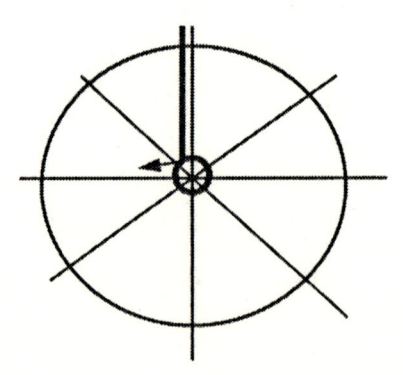

- Pin one end to the frame and bring the strip to the center. Then begin working around the center with the other end, going over and under each spoke in turn, ending with the added strip. Continue weaving in a spiral, going completely around once more.
- If you are using the same weight and size of fabric for both the "spokes" (warp) and the weaving, you will need to add another set of warp/spokes about every other row. (If using fabrics of different weights or widths, you'll have to use your own judgement about when to add more spokes.)

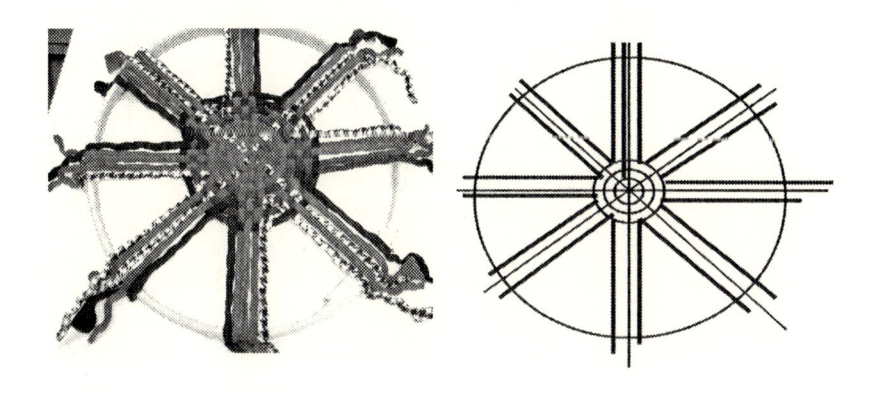

Spokes are added in a 'V' pattern alongside the most recent set of spokes. Always add spokes all of the way around the rug at the same time. Pin one end of the new strip to the rim of the frame. Loop the center of the strip over the last round of weaving. Pin the other end to the frame just inside the next spoke.
- Fold the strand over the previous row of weaving, and then look carefully at it. You will notice that one end passes over the weaving, and one end passes under the weaving. Place the ends of the new spoke so that they continue the weaving pattern. For example, the correct placement of a spoke is to have the end passing over the weaving strand pinned next to the previous spoke which passed underneath the weaving strand.
- You will need to add new sets of spokes to the wheel at regular intervals: usually for every 2-3 rounds of weaving. The spacing of the spokes will be determined by the relative weights of the fabrics

used for the warp and the weaving. Just remember that you want the weaving to be as even as possible.

- As the weaving progresses, you will need to add more weaving strip. How the new strip is attached depends on the shape of the weaving strip itself. For strips with flat profiles, the easiest method is to sew the strip directly to the warp strands. At any warp strand that the weaving strip will go over, sew the end of the new strip directly to the warp. Then weave over that spot with the old strip. When the old strip passes underneath the next warp strand, sew the end of the strip directly to the warp and clip it off. Weaving is then continued with the new strip, which will cover the seam where the old strip was sewn down. For weaving strips with a round profile (like double-folded wool, or T-shirt cottons formed into tubes), a new weaving strip is sewn directly to the end of the old weaving strip using the regular bias joint.
- As the weaving grows, stop occasionally and readjust the fabric rounds with your fingers. If you find that an added spoke is pulling the weaving out of place, loosen it just a little, and readjust the weaving so that you don't have a hole in the rug.
- When your weaving has reached the edge of the frame, it is time to finish off the rug and remove it from the frame. Take the end of the weaving strip and tuck it between a spoke and the previous round of weaving so that the raw end is completely hidden. Then sew the end in place.
- Using a needle and thread, and hiding your stitches, sew around the outside edge of the weaving, making sure that every spoke is sewn firmly to the last round of the weaving.
- When the sewing is complete, pull out the T-pins which attach the rug to the frame. Lay the rug on a flat surface. Trim the ends

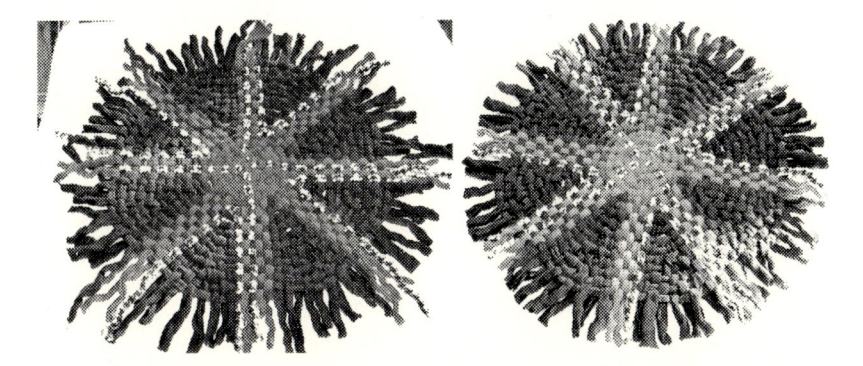

of the spokes evenly around the outside of the weaving. The ends should be at least two inches long and not more than six inches. (Different fabrics will look best with either long or shorter ends, so with the first trimming leave the ends a bit longer than you think they should be. Then if they need to be shortened or evened up you will have enough strip to do it.) The rug above is shown before and after the ends of the strips have been trimmed.

- If you have a problem where your weaving wasn't as snug as it should have been, the problem will show up after you have taken the rug off the frame. To fix the problem, lay the rug on a table, and adjust the weaving strips so that they are as even as possible. Then using hidden stitches, sew along the spokes to hold the weaving strips where they should be.
- If your rug doesn't lay perfectly flat when you first take it off the frame don't panic. Usually all that is needed is to let the rug lay on a flat surface overnight to let the fabric strips "relax." If the rug still isn't laying exactly as you'd like, then you can steam it until it lies perfectly flat. (With a wool rug that you want to exhibit, steaming is always a good idea anyway. It will flatten out the fringe and make the weaving appear more regular.)

The Fine Points of Wagon Wheel Rugs

Nearly all of the wagon wheel rugs that I've ever seen use the same fabrics for all of the initial "spokes" of the wheel. That design allows for a progression of colors in each "V" between the spokes as the weaving continues and spokes are added. Don't feel constrained to use only one fabric for the spokes if you want to experiment with different looks. The example rug uses two different colors of wool for the initial spokes, with the lightest color repeated only four times in an added spoke. Notice how the placement adds interest to the rug design.

Older wagon wheel rugs used only solid colors in the strands for both the warp and the weaving, which accents the texture of the rug. Prints and plaids will disguise (somewhat) the texture, and are particularly effective when the same fabric is used for both purposes.

Making an Oval Wagon Wheel Rug

It is fairly easy to make a Wagon Wheel rug in an oval shape. Just think of the oval as two half-circles, separated by a section of straight weaving. The initial setup of the warp is different, but the weaving and finishing of the ovals are the same as for the round rugs.

To make an oval, you will need a frame of the appropriate size of course, and will need to know the dimensions of the frame opening to be able to place the weaving strands for the center section. The rounded ends of the oval will extend one half of the total width into the rug. For example, if your frame opening measures 3 feet by 5 feet, one half of the width would be 1½ feet. Mark that length on the sides of the frame to use as a guide for placing the center warp strands.

- Pin the center warp strand in place first. This is the strand that runs the length of the rug. Then, following the guide marks, pin the strands for the center section of straight weaving. These strands will pass alternately under and over the center strand. (You can also pin the weaving strands first, and then weave the center strand through them.)

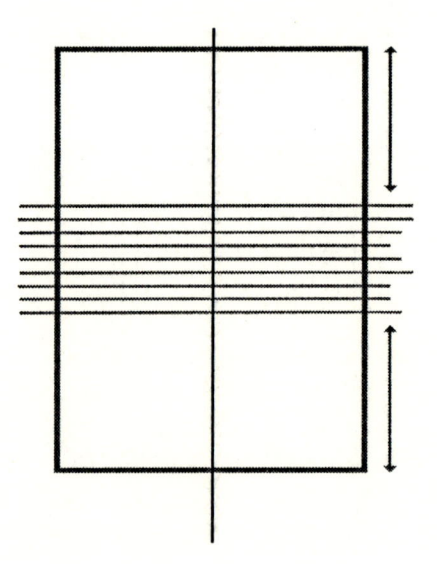

Center strand

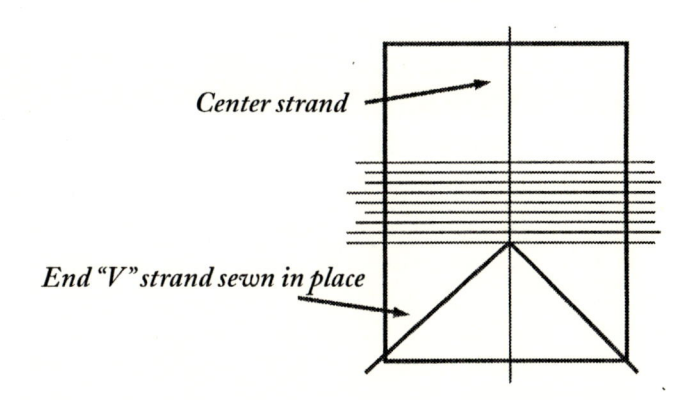

End "V" strand sewn in place

- At each end, one long strand is pinned to a corner, sewn to the center strand and then pinned to the opposite corner, as shown in the drawing.

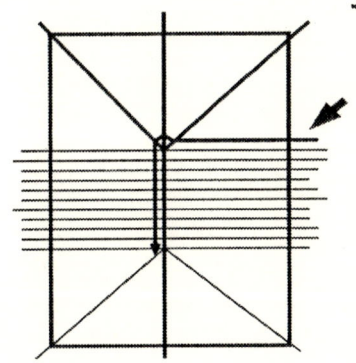

- In order to have an odd number of strands for weaving, begin by pinning the weaving strand next to any of the existing strands. Bring its end to the center of the rug and begin weaving.

- Additional spokes and weaving strands are added just as for the round wagon wheel shape.

PART IV: WEIRD AND WONDERFUL WARPS

CHAPTER 17
Twisted Warp Techniques

The twisted warp rugs all appear to be "twined" rugs from a surface examination, but they are actually the reverse of twining, since it is the warp, not the weft strands, which are twisted. The advantage to twisted warp rugs (especially done on flat frames) is that they can be made in much less time than a twined rug.

With all of the twisted warp methods, the technique of creating the rug is the same, but the process of installing the twisted warps is specific to the type of frame used. As the name implies, the warp strands are twisted in pairs as they are put on the frame. The rug structure is created by lacing through the twists, back and forth, in rows across the warp. The tricky part of twisted warp rugs is that the spacing of the twists has to be proportionate to the size of the material used for the lacing.

If the warps are twisted at ½-inch intervals (two twists to the inch), the lacing material should be a stout string or heavy cord. The 6-ply linen sold for lacing rugs together is a good choice.

Twisted Warp Techniques

If the warps are twisted at ¾- or one-inch intervals, the lacing material should be a cotton fabric 1½ inches wide and double-folded. A cording of approximately the same weight can also be used.

If the warps are twisted at 1½- inch intervals, the rug can be laced with a heavy fabric. This option should really only be used when the entire rug is made of the same heavy fabric. For example, if the warp is composed of wool 1½-inches wide (which should be double-folded), the rug can be laced with wool of the same width. This procedure is most effective in creating fringes on four sides, rather than working back and forth in the lacing.

Because there is so much lacing involved in these rugs, the right lacing tool will make the job much easier. For light cording or linen, use a bodkin which is ski-shaped with two holes such as is used for lacing braided rugs together. For lacing with fabrics use a lacing needle about six inches long—preferably one with a curved, blunted tip. For lacing with heavy fabrics, use a pinch-style bodkin, such as is used for inserting elastic into a waist band, or a large safety pin.

Using a Flat Frame with Twisted Warps

Any flat frame can be used, but there will be tack or staple holes, so if you have an expensive hooking frame, don't use it with this method. Buy or build a basic frame instead.

The twisted warp rugs all work the best using fabric strip, which is round in profile. Flat, wide strip will not cooperate, nor will the finished rug look neat. The best fabrics for the twisted warp rugs are heavy wool, cut 1½ inches wide and double-folded or T-shirt knits cut 1½ to 2 inches wide and curled into a tube. (See the Handbook section for more about using T-shirt knits.) Unfolded cotton strip will have a tendency to overlap as the warp is twisted, making it difficult to lace the rug together, but it can be used. Pre-washed cotton fabrics should be cut or torn two to three inches wide for use on the flat frame. The wider the strips, the heavier the rug will be.

Cut the warp strands to the length of the rug plus about 1/3 to allow for the twisting. (For a rug three feet long, cut the warp strands at least four feet long). Always check the measurement by twisting a pair of the strands since very heavy fabrics will shorten more than light fabrics in the twisting.

Measure the inside opening of the frame. For twists spaced at ½-inch intervals, double the number to calculate the number of times each warp pair will be twisted. For example, if the inside opening measures 34 inches, each warp pair will need to be twisted 68 times to achieve a spacing at ½-inch. (For one inch spacing, use the frame measurement, and for 1½-inch spacing, divide the measurement by 1.5 for the number of twists needed.)

Using a staple gun or stout tacks (not upholstery tacks), attach the first pair of warp strands to the end of the frame. When attaching pairs of warp strands, always place one strand directly on top of the other. Twist them around each other for the number of times that were calculated above, then staple or tack the warp strands to the other end of the frame.

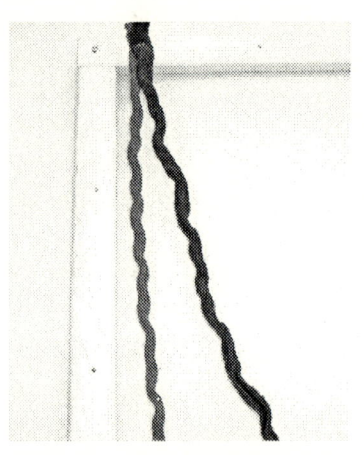

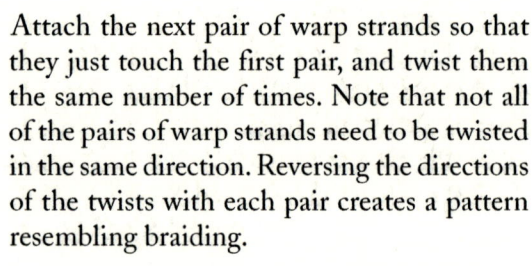

Attach the next pair of warp strands so that they just touch the first pair, and twist them the same number of times. Note that not all of the pairs of warp strands need to be twisted in the same direction. Reversing the directions of the twists with each pair creates a pattern resembling braiding.

Continue attaching pairs of warp strands until they fill the width of the frame opening. When all of the warp pairs are attached, adjust the position of the first and last twists so that they line up. Baste across these first twists to hold them in place in line across the rug.

- Attach the end of the lacing strip to the first warp strand with a safety pin. Outside the pin, leave a section of fabric strip about 10 inches long, if lacing with fabric. Leave a section of cording that is the width of the rug. For heavy fabrics, leave the length of the desired side fringe.
- Work the lacing under the first row of twists across the rug. The first question that everyone asks is "How do I tell where the first twist is?" If you attached your warp pairs one on top of the other, it is easy to spot the first twist, since it is where the strand on the bottom first appears at the top. Take a look at the photograph on the bottom of the previous page. The staples securing the pair are visible. The first twist is where the second color is on top just past the staple.
- Lace completely across the row. Pull the lacing up snugly so that all of the twisted strands are held together. If you allowed a little too much space between the pairs, the twisted warp will pull in. For these sorts of rugs, that is fine. The lacing should hold the warp pairs firmly together, and can be adjusted for a straight edge when the warp is removed from the frame.

- Insert the lacing needle or bodkin into the second row of twists and lace across to the other side. In the photo at right, notice that the lacing is nearly complete, and at the end of each row of lacing a small loop of slack has been left in the lacing. These loops are pulled through for final shaping of the rug, just as for the freeform shaping described in Chapter 8.
- Continue up the rug, lacing through each row of twists. Add on lacing strip by sewing as needed. Securely tie on more cord if lacing with cording. Hide the knots under a twist.
- When the rug is completely laced, go back and adjust the lacings to get a straight edge on the rug. Final lacing adjustment can be made after the rug is removed from the frame.
- Baste across the warp strands with needle and thread. The line of basting should be between the first row of lacing and the frame. Baste both ends of the rug. Remove the staples or tacks holding the twisted warps, then re-lace through the next-to-last row at both ends. If lacing with cording, tie the cording to the lacing under a twist and clip off any excess. If lacing with fabric strip, sew the end of the lacing strip in place under a twist. (Note if lacing with heavy fabric, forming side fringes, you do not need to relace.)

Before removing the staples or tacks holding the warp strands, double-check that the basting holding the first twist is still intact. If not, re-baste any section that did not hold. Then remove the tacks or staples holding the warp to the frame. Hand sew a line of back stitches just outside the first and last twists to hold them solidly in place. Then remove the basting stitches. If you used heavy fabric to make fringes on the sides of the rug, also sew them by hand to the last row of warp. Trim the fringed ends (and sides) evenly to the desired length.

If your rug has a tendency to cup at the ends, the lacing was pulled a little too tight, but the rug will be fine anyway. Use a dampened dishtowel and a hot iron to steam the rug flat, and let it dry completely before use.

Using a Pegged Frame with Twisted Warps

You can make a twisted warp rug on a pegged frame very similarly to the flat frame if you want to have fringed ends. Just tie or sew the warp strips together on opposite sets of pegs and twist them just as for a flat frame.

Using a pegged frame, you can make a twisted warp rug with four finished sides instead. This is not, however, a beginner method. The warp is put on the frame in a modified continuous warp and then laced together. The disadvantage of a continuous twisted warp is that with a fabric warp, the rug will only be one color, unless you take the time to sew lots of different colors together as you make the warp. (The advantage of the continuous warp is an even more advanced technique, where the warp is twisted using a heavy thread or cording, and the lacing is done with strips of heavy fabrics. The warp is not prominent and it is the fabric used for lacing through the twists that shows in the rug.)

Rigging a twisted warp on a pegged frame takes a little trial-and-error to get the exact measure for each warp pair, so you will want to keep notes. For your first piece, I strongly suggest using the square foot pegged frame in Part I, since it is small and easily handled. Once you are comfortable with the procedure, you can switch to a larger frame.

Have the fabric for the warp cut, joined and double-folded. Use 1½-inch cotton fabric for both the twisted warp and for the lacing on your first practice rug. Then you can branch out to other materials. Note that using unfolded strip for this rug will just make it hard to find and lace the twists in the warp, and is not recommended for a first rug.

- Tie the end of the warp fabric to a corner peg of the square foot frame. Pull a loop of the warp across the frame so that it is about one-third longer than the width of the frame. Loosely tie the warp to the second peg. Then twist the loop of warp strands 24 times for a ½-inch interval on a one foot frame. If the end loop of the warp pair will just slip over the peg, you're all set. More likely, though the twisted warp will be either too long or too short to exactly reach the opposite peg. Untwist the warp, and adjust the knot that is over the second peg. If your warp pair was too long, shorten the length of the warp. If it was too short, add a little length to the warp. Twist the warp strands again. Repeat adjusting the length of the warp until, after twisting, the last loop will just slip over the opposite peg. 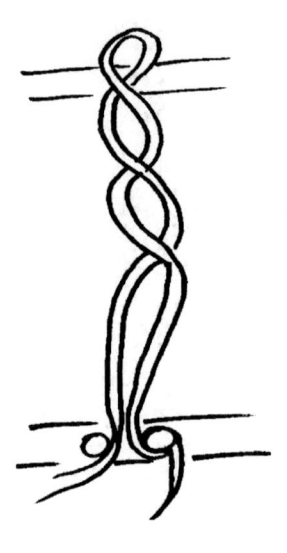
- Then untwist the warp one more time and measure it. That will give you the length needed for all of the warp sections across the frame.

- Note that the end of the warp strand is tied off on the last peg. Leave a fairly long tail—about the width of the rug—to weave back in after the lacing is complete.
- The rug is laced together working back and forth in continuous rows, beginning with the first row of twists and one end and working to the other end under each row of twists.
- Tie the lacing to the first peg, leaving enough of a tail to work 1 ½ times the rug width. For the first rug, use 1½-inch cotton strip (preferably double-folded) for the lacing. As you lace, don't pull the strip so tightly that the twisted warps bunch up.

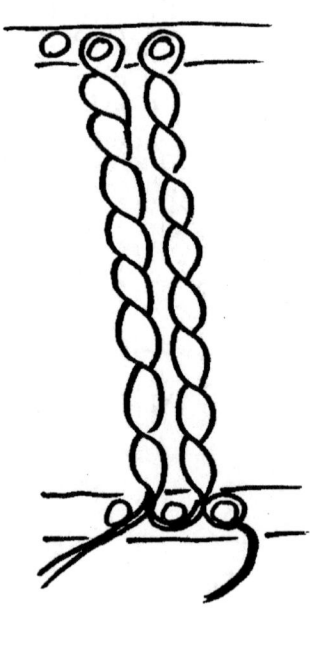

They should lay snugly together, just touching. You will occasionally need to sew on additional strip for the lacing.
- Finishing a continuous twisted warp is a little different than most other pegged rugs, since the loops over the pegs themselves will also need to be twisted and laced. Remove the loop nearest the lacing strip from its peg, twist it in the same direction as the rest of the warp, and lace through it. Continue across the end lacing each loop as it is removed from the frame. When that end is laced, work the lacing back through the previous row under about half the rug width and sew the end down. Repeat the removal process at the other end of the frame.
- The tails of the warp are then laced under several twists also, and sewn in place.

Using a Hanging Frame with Twisted Warps

This technique for creating twisted warp rugs looks the easiest, but has its complexities as well. The warp is fairly quickly made using yard goods or sheets. For new fabrics, pre-wash before cutting to remove the sizing. You will need a section of fabric that is approximately twice the desired length of the rug. Light cottons, such as calicos work the best. The fabric is folded in half lengthwise and the ends overlapped and sewn to create a continuous circle. There should be about a ¼-inch seam allowance. Sew two straight seams along the joining. Trim off the selvage if it doesn't match the print. Note that the selvage edges should not be included in the seams. Ideally, the fabrics should be sewn with the cut edges (not selvage edges), which will allow the strips to be cut parallel to the selvage. That is the direction with the strongest threads.

The fabric tube is cut into strips, usually two inches wide. When the cutting is completed, you will have lots of fabric loops. If your fabric was about 44 inches wide, you will have 20 or 21 loops, which will make a rug about 20 or 21 inches wide. For wider rugs, create more loops the same way, making sure that they are all the same length. Using loops of several different colors will, of course, create stripes in the rug. Another interesting option is to make the fabric tubes of two or more different fabrics, and then cut the loops.

The hanging frame consists of two dowels—one for the top and one for the bottom. The dowels should be at least ½-inch in diameter. Work on a flat surface while you twist the warp loops and put them on the dowels.

- The formula for determining how many twists to put into the warp is: the length of the warp loop, divided by the width of the warp. For example, if you used a two-yard piece of fabric to sew into a tube, the loops cut from that fabric will be about 36 inches long. If you cut each warp two inches wide, you will need to twist each warp loop 18 times. (36/2 = 16)
- Slide the end of one fabric loop over a dowel, twist it the number of times calculated above, and slide the other end of the loop over the second dowel. Repeat until all of the fabric loops are twisted and put on the dowels. Note that not all of the warp loops need to be twisted the same direction. 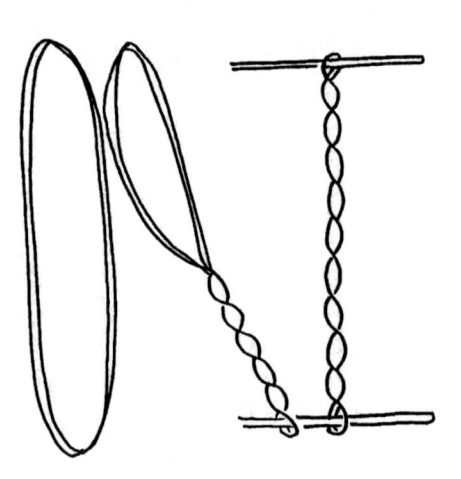 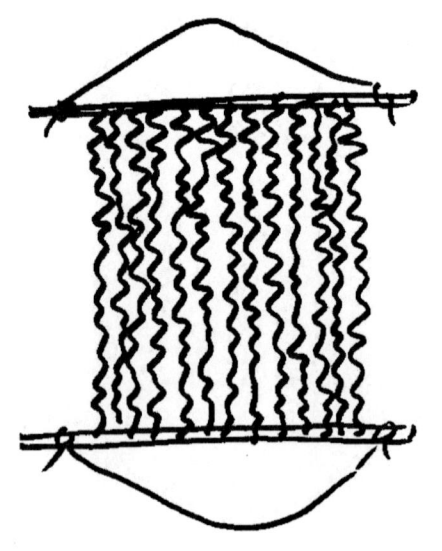
- Tie a heavy cord or piece of fabric strip on both ends of each dowel to form hangers for the frame. Hang the frame on the wall with a nail or picture frame hanger, or use an over-the-door clothes hanger to hang the frame behind a door. Add some weight to the bottom dowel. It should be a couple of pounds, and actually a pair of men's work boots fill the bill nicely since they can be attached to the lower rod by the shoestrings.

Twisted Warp Techniques

- Let the warp rest overnight, with the weights, to allow it to stretch if it wants to.
- For the lacing you can use cotton fabric cut one inch wide (for a fairly light rug) or up to two inches wide for a heavier rug. The lacing strip does not have to be double-folded, but the lacing will go more easily if it is.
- Use a lacing needle or large safety pin on the lacing fabric. Work the lacing strip through the first row of twists next to the dowel. You can begin either at the top or the bottom dowel. Leave a tail of the lacing strip that is 1½ times the width of the rug. That tail will be laced through the loops on the dowel when the rug is ready to finish off.
- When you have laced the first row of twists, adjust the position of the warp strands so that they are evenly spaced, fitting snugly against each other.
- Then work the lacing back across the rug under the second row of twists. Then the third row and so on. When you run low on lacing strip, sew on more using the overlapping bias joint, and continue lacing. Adjust the warp strands after each row of lacing to keep a straight edge on the rug.
- Note that when you have laced about half of the rug, you can turn the frame over to keep working at the most convenient height.
- When you have finished lacing the last row of twists before the dowel, you will want to take the frame down so that you can do the final lacing on a flat surface. Slide the dowel out of the first loop nearest the lacing strip, and lace through the loop, making sure to hold it so it can't untwist in the lacing. Slip the dowel out of the second loop, and lace through it the same way. Do the same across, until all of the loops on the dowel have been removed and laced.
- Take the lacing strip back to the previous row of loops, and lace about halfway across. Sew the end of the lacing strip in place, and clip off any excess.
- Repeat the process to remove the dowel at the other end, and the rug is completed.

CHAPTER 18
Spider Web Warp

This is a novel way of putting a warp on a flat frame, and in many ways rugs made this way will seem to resemble the wagon wheel rug. This is not a warp that should be used with weaving though. Instead, it should be used only with the non-tensioning methods in Part I of the book, which use the ½-inch warp spacing.

This warp is best used with square (or nearly square) frames. It can be applied to a rectangular frame, if the length and width don't have a difference of more than one foot. (A 3' X 4' frame will work, but not a 3' X 5' frame.) In learning to use the spider web warping, start small—with a 2' X 2' frame, or smaller—while you learn to handle the warp strands. The key to success with this warp is an even tension throughout the warp, which takes some practice.

There are three distinct parts to rugs made with this warp. The "backbone" which supports the warp strands, and is attached to the frame. The warp, which is attached to the "backbone" but not the frame. The rug surface fabric is attached to the warp.

The "backbones" of the warp are two pairs of strands, twisted around each other. The fabrics for these must be firmly woven, so that they do not stretch, which will loosen the warp. Appropriate fabrics include cotton, wool or synthetic, and all should be cut 1½ inches wide and double-folded.

For the warp, cotton or cotton blend fabrics are ideal. They should also be cut 1½ inches wide and double-folded. Because the warp is one continuous strand through the entire spider web, sections of warp strip will need to be sewn on as the warp gets larger. The warp will be entirely covered, so you can sew the ends together with hand stitches, or use the regular bias-joint.

Spider Web Warp

The rug surface stitches (with any of the non-tensioning methods) can be made of any fabric that is suited to the method itself. In the rug surface, you can mix and match fabrics and techniques for different textures.

- Begin by measuring the opening of your frame. You will need to know the distance from one corner to the opposite on the diagonal. For the example rug, a frame with an opening of 24 inches by 18 inches is used. The diagonal measurement is 29½ inches. The diagonal measurement is always rounded up to the nearest whole number, which for the example frame is 30. That is how many twists will be on each of the four backbones from the **corner to the center** of the rug.

- Use a staplegun or strong tacks to secure the ends of two "backbone" strands to one corner. Then twist them together, counting as you go. Each time the fabrics reverse positions counts as one twist.

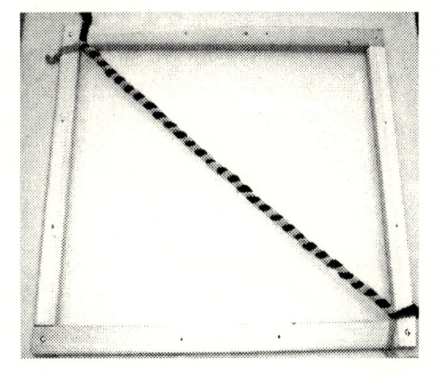

- The first backbone will reach from a corner to the middle to the opposite corner, so it will require twice the number calculated above. In the sample rug, the number calculated to reach the middle was 30, so this first backbone has 60 twists in it.

- When you have made the correct number of twists, staple or tack the ends of the strips to the frame as shown.

- Count back along the twists to get to the middle of the first backbone, to find the middle. In the sample rug, the middle twist will be number 30. Mark the middle twist with a pin or a piece of thread.

- Attach the strands for the second backbone to an empty corner, and begin twisting it. When you reach the middle number (30 in the example), thread *one* strand through the marked middle twist of the first backbone.

- Then continue twisting the backbone fabric until it reaches the other end. Use one less than the calculated number of twists (29 in the example), since the connection to the first backbone also counts as one twist. Staple or tack the ends of the final backbone to the frame. Note that the backbone sections should be firmly twisted so that they don't sag to the tabletop, but instead hold themselves at the level of the frame. To tighten up a backbone, just pull the ends of the strands in opposite directions and then reattach them to the frame.

- To attach the warp to the backbone, begin at the very center where the two backbones cross. Slip the end of the warp strand into the crossing, and sew it firmly in place with hand stitches. Cut off about five or six feet of the warp to begin, and thread the loose end into a lacing needle.

Spider Web Warp 143

- The warp is attached to the backbones by lacing it underneath each twist. Begin with the first twist that is next to the place where the two backbones cross each other. Work under the first twist on all of the backbones until you get back to the first lacing. Then move up to the second twist, and lace the warp through all four of those. Then the third twist, and so on around. The lacing is done in this spiral fashion, continuing until all of the warp is applied—up to the final twist in the backbone strips.
- When a section of warp strand is used up, sew on an additional length, and continue lacing around. When you reach the final twist, sew the end of the warp directly to the backbone, inside the final twist.
- When the warping is finished, you're all ready to begin with the rug surface. Use any of the non-tensioning methods in Part I of

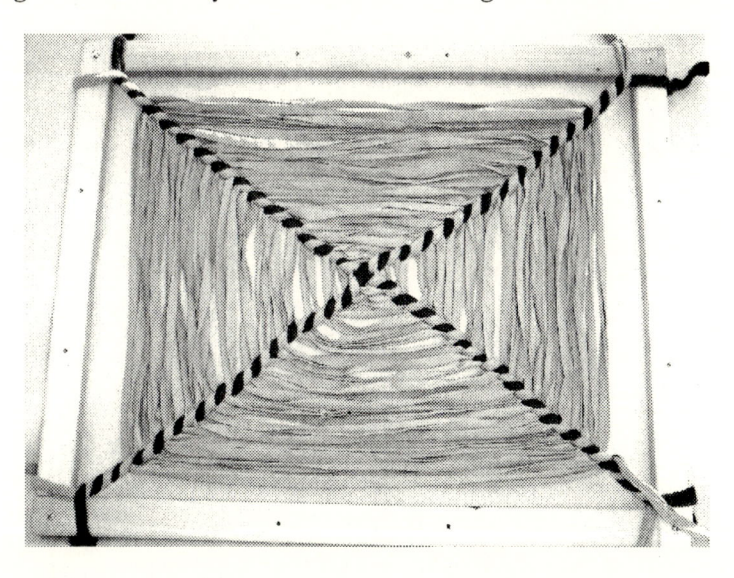

the book, which use a ½-inch warp spacing. When the rug surface is done, sew the end twists of the backbones together, so that one crosses over the top of the other, and both ends point back to the center of the rug. Tuck the ends of the strands under a twist of the same color and sew the end in place. Clip off the excess length of each strand. Finish off by making several sewing stitches all of the way through the end of the backbone to reinforce it and make sure that any tendency to untwist is prevented.

    Notice that for the backbones in the example rug, I used two very different colors of fabric (light weight wool). The two different colors make the twists easier to see and to count. In the lacing it also makes it easy to know which twist is to be laced next. I really suggest that you also use two different colored fabrics for the backbones, especially on your first rug.

    The calculations in the general directions will give you a ½-inch warp spacing. If you want a wider or narrower warp spacing when using alternate materials, you will need to modify the calculation. For example, if you wanted a one-inch warp spacing, the actual measurement of the diagonal (in inches) would be how many twists would be needed in each backbone. For a 1/3-inch warp spacing, the measurement of the diagonal would be multiplied by three to give the total number of twists, and that number would be divided by two to get the number of twists needed from the corner to the center.

    Because the spider web warp is not as tight as warps on pegged frames, it is easy to overfill the warp strands with the rows of the rug surface. If you do that, the edges of the rug won't be straight—instead they will round to the outside—giving the rug an almost round or oval shape. Don't worry that the shape is a mistake—you can do it intentionally for just that particular effect.

CHAPTER 19
The "Fifth Stick" Frame

In all of the weaving references that I have seen, primitive frames are depicted as four sticks lashed together at the corners, forming a high-low arrangement, and the warp is tied to the two high sticks. Of course, with a tied warp, weaving creates tension and each warp strand would have had to have been untied, and re-tied at intervals.

I am going to go out on a limb and postulate that our pre-historic ancestors would have used a fifth stick to eliminate the tensioning problem simply. In studying the pre-historic textile references that are available, two things have repeatedly struck me as true. The first is that pre-historic peoples were astonishingly resourceful at using the materials available and they were very good at creating and using simple tools. The second is that there are some basic textile constructions and techniques that appear to be "intuitive"—appearing in places far distant from each other. These "intuitive" methods seem to be the human answer when faced with the same problem. This fifth-stick method of weaving seems to me to be such an "intuitive" solution to the problem of the warp tension created by weaving.

The "fifth stick" method works fine with a flat frame made of finished lumber, but I am going to illustrate the method with a primitive high-low frame, modified just for the technique. I often hear from youth leaders and teachers interested in teaching weaving with simple materials that don't cost much. This primitive frame can be made with five straight sticks, tied as show, and the weaving done with recycled clothing. If you are using a flat frame, which you already have, just skip down to the instructions for warping the frame.

To construct the modified high-low frame, select four straight sticks at least ½-inch in diameter for a small frame, and an inch or more in diameter for frames that are longer or wider than 24 inches. (Lacking a source of sticks, use dowels, and for little-bitty classroom projects, use wooden pencils.) The corners of the frames are lashed together, by wrapping with stout string or cord in a figure-eight pattern. The lashing must be tight enough—and with enough wraps to hold the frame reasonably square.

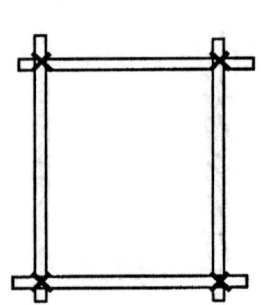

The end pieces of the frame are lashed on opposite sides of the frame. The end which is above the side pieces will face the weaver, and the end which is below the frame acts as a prop at the farther end.

The "fifth stick" is attached to the frame using one cord at each end. The center of the cord is placed over the fifth stick. Both ends of the cord are brought underneath the frame to the outside, and tied above the fifth stick. I use a short piece of fabric strip for this tie.

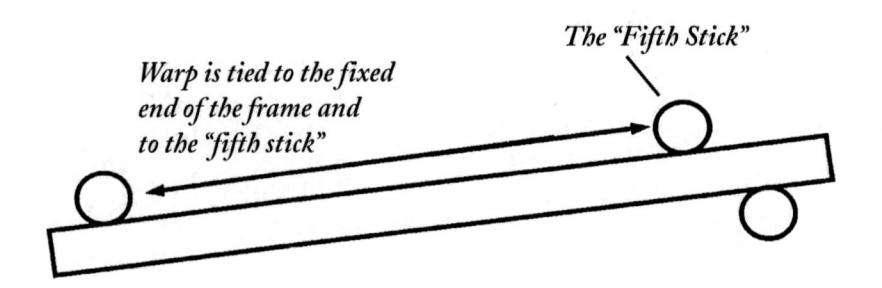

Warp is tied to the fixed end of the frame and to the "fifth stick"

The "Fifth Stick"

The "Fifth Stick" Frame 147

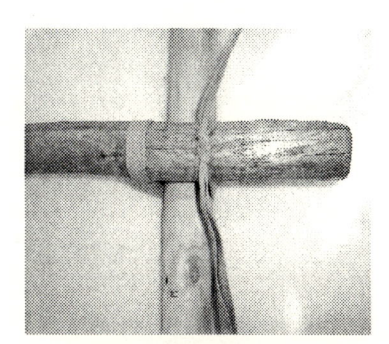

With the "fifth stick" on top of the frame, lay a length of cord or fabric strip on top of the fifth stick, and pass the ends under the frame. Bring the ends of the strip up and tie them around the end of the fifth stick.

The warp is secured to the frame by tying it to the frame itself on the end facing the weaver, and to the "fifth stick." Light cotton fabrics cut one inch wide make a good warp for a rug, or a stout string or cord can be used for the warp on smaller weavings or wall hangings. The warp needs to be tied with an even tension, but should not be drum-head tight. If you are working with children, don't worry too much about the warp tension since you can make some adjustments to the warp after the weaving is off the frame. The thing to watch for on a tied warp is one or two strands that are significantly tighter than the rest of the warp. They will have the most strain on them as tension increases on the warp and, particularly with a string warp, those strands may break.

The weft can be of any sort of fabric and can be cut varying widths if desired for special effects. Of course, yarns can also be mixed in or "found" materials including plastic grocery sacks cut open, grasses, feathers, *etc*.

Begin weaving at the end of the frame—not at the "fifth stick." Any weave can be used, but tabby (over one, under one) is the best choice for rug projects. As each row is woven, use your fingers to adjust the row firmly in place near the previous row. To avoid "waisting" make sure that the weft makes a small arc across the row before it is pushed into place.

When the warp strands tighten significantly, it is time to adjust the "fifth stick" to reposition the warp strands and relieve the tension. Usually, by moving the cord holding the fifth stick on the underside of the frame, the stick will slide a little at a time. If your cord is tied very tightly, you may need to loosen the knot just a little to allow the fifth stick to move. Do not untie the cord completely—just loosen the knot holding it.

Then continue weaving until the warp tightens up again, and reposition the fifth stick. When the weaving has filled the space available, the weaving can be removed from the loom by untying the warp strands from the frame and the fifth stick. If a string warp was used, the strings can be tied to form fringes. For a cloth warp, sew a line of stitches along the last row of weaving, securing the warp strands to the weaving. Remove one end of the weaving at a time for the hand sewing. Cloth warp strands can also be worked back into the weaving by folding them over the last row of weaving and threading them in a line back down the path of the warp.

CHAPTER 20
Suspended Warps on Pegged Frames

If you have a frame with wooden pegs spaced one inch apart, it is easy to put on a continuous warp with a spacing of one or ½ inches by the simple process of wrapping the warp strand around the existing pegs. To have an evenly spaced warp at ¼-inch, however, a "suspended" warp is used. This warping pattern is called suspended since alternate strands aren't attached directly to the pegs at all. Instead, they are held in place by other warp strands.

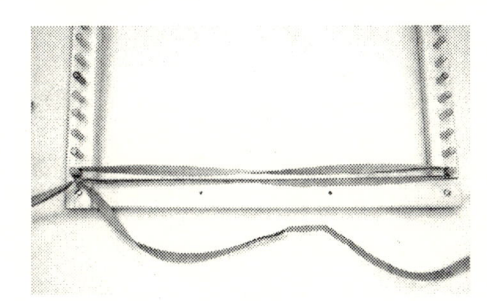

- Begin by tying a single loop of warp, which will just fit over the first peg on each side of the frame. The end of the warp fabric should come from underneath the frame.

- Reach between the two strands of the loop and pull some fabric strip to the top.

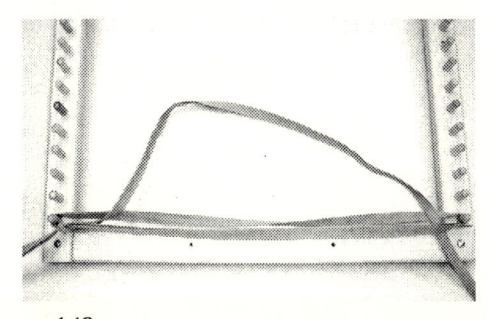

- Use your hands to stretch the warp strand to the sides of the frame. (In the illustration, two hooks are used to illustrate where your fingers should hold the warp to position it properly.)

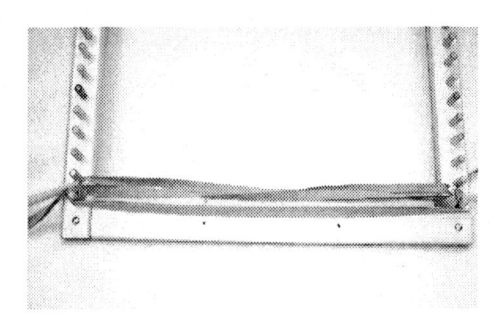

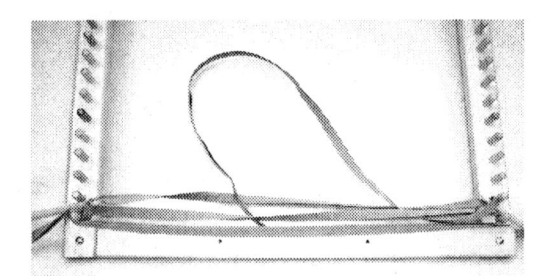

- Then pull another loop of warp through the last loop, and with this one, lay it over the tops of the next set of pegs on each side. Note that the previous warp strand is held in place by this one, and if it needs to be adjusted for tension or placement, now is the time to do it.

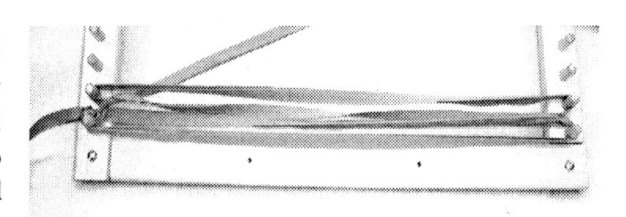

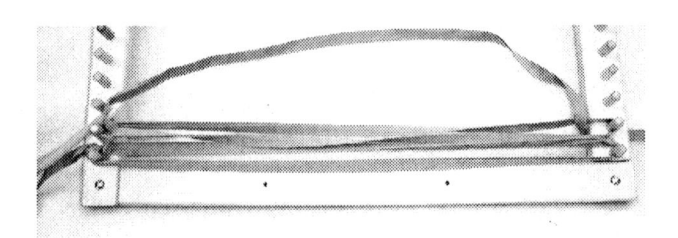

- Pull up another loop of warp between the previous two warp strands. Hold this one in place with your fingers.

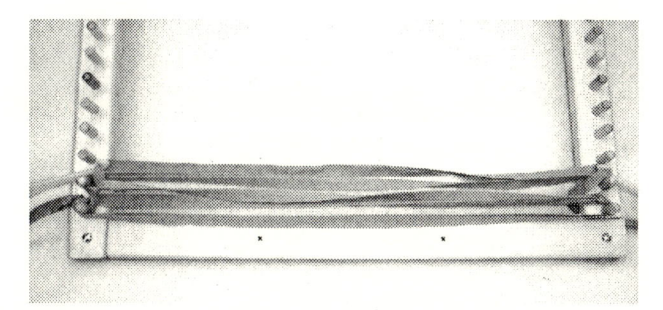

- Pull up the next loop of warp from between the two previous warp strands and set it in place over the next set of pegs.
- The warping proceeds by alternating a "suspended" warp strand with a strand placed over the next set of pegs.
- When you reach the final set of pegs, tie off the end of the warp strand to the warp, not the peg.

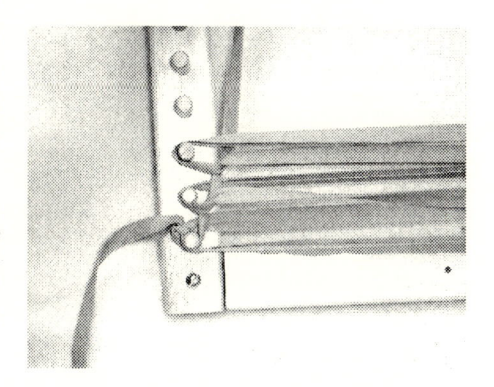

The suspended warp takes a little practice to do evenly, but because it is a continuous warp, you can adjust the tension even after the frame is completely warped. Just work any excess slack along from strand to strand, and re-tie the end of the warp.

Because of the looping of the strands in the suspended warp, it cannot be used for free-form shaping of rugs, but it is fine for any other application. The ¼-inch warp is really only necessary for locker hooking with fabrics, or if you plan to use a light material for the rug surface (such as yarns).

A suspended warp can also be used for weaving on a pegged frame. See the instructions for using a pegged frame as a "walking frame" in Chapter 13.

CHAPTER 21
The Cheater's Warp

With a flat frame, rugs can be made by using a single piece of cloth to form all of the warp strands. This "cheater's warp" is easy to put on, but takes some time to make sure that the slits separating the warp strands are precisely made—and all the same width. The best type of fabric to use for the warp is a heavy denim, canvas or duck (at least 10 ounces weight). The fabric has to be quite strongly woven to work well on a flat frame.

The disadvantage of the cheater's warp is that it will make a rug that isn't completely reversible, since the warp fabric will be hemmed on the back side of the rug. Otherwise, the simplicity of the method makes it a good choice for a rug maker with limited time.

The cheater's warp is looser than regular warp methods, so it can sometimes stretch after it comes off of the frame when non-tensioning methods are used. To accommodate the stretch, you can include weaving in the design, but the warp will show, which may not be desirable. Generally, the easiest thing to do is to work with a non-tensioning method, and plan on adding more rows once the warp is off of the frame, if they are needed.

To minimize the stretch in the warp fabric, plan to cut the warp strands in the shortest dimension (the width) of the rug. Cut the fabric for the warp an inch or two wider than the warp will be and long enough to wrap the end of the fabric around the frame to the back side for attachment. Lay the warp fabric on a flat surface and then lay the frame face down on the fabric. The fabric should more than cover the opening on the frame.

Bring the end of the fabric around the frame and staple or tack it to the frame itself. Beginning with the center of the fabric at both ends, pull the fabric as tightly as you can as it is tacked or stapled down. Then work gradually to the corners, keep the fabric tight to the frame as you go.

When the fabric is securely attached, turn the frame over. Use a yardstick to mark guide dots every ½-inch along the edge of the frame opening. To make sure that the dots align at both ends of the warp, have the first dot marked the same distance from the outer edge of the frame.

- When all of the guide dots are marked. Use a pencil or pen to draw lines connecting the guide dots. A yardstick works well to keep the lines straight between the dots because most yardsticks are a little flexible. The warp fabric will sag as you draw your guidelines, so push down on the yardstick to be able to draw a consistently straight line between the dots.
- After all of the guidelines are drawn, the warp fabric is ready to cut into slits. I usually use a razor knife (utility knife) just to start the cuts and then a good pair of scissors for the actual cutting. Scissors are much easier to control. The cuts in the fabric should extend only across the actual opening of the frame.
- Cut carefully along all of the guidelines. At the outer edges there will be an extra-wide piece (or narrow, or irregular). That edge piece is cut off of the frame at both ends, leaving only the even warp cuts in the middle.

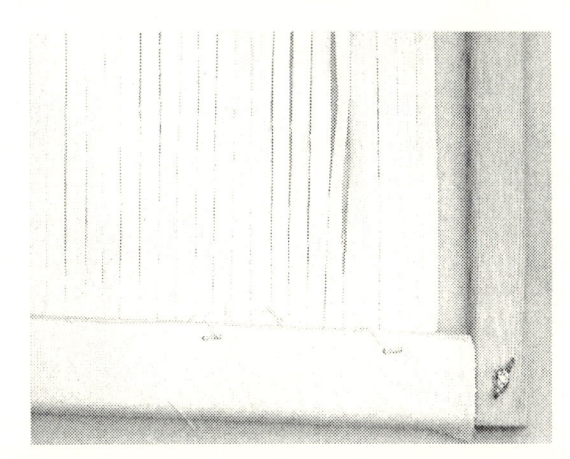

The back side of the frame with the cheater's warp in place. Note that the staples securing the warp fabric on on the back side of the frame, not on the edges.

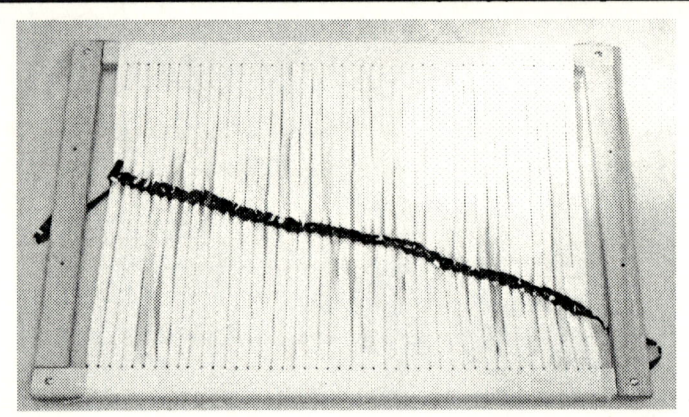

- At this point, the warp is ready to use. Select any of the non-tensioning techniques in Part I that use ½-inch warp spacing. You can also use weaving for part of the rug surface to tighten the warp strands if you like (and if you don't mind the warp strands showing).

If you plan to have a design in your rug, draw the main elements directly on the warp fabric and fill in the sections in any order that is convenient. Completely fill in each design area, making sure that the rows forming the rug surface are closely packed together.

The cheater's warp does not allow stitches or rows to slide as easily as regular warp strands, and if the rows are forced to move very far, the fabric strips can fray and weaken. In the photographs below, the same rug is shown in process with various elements in process and after completion.

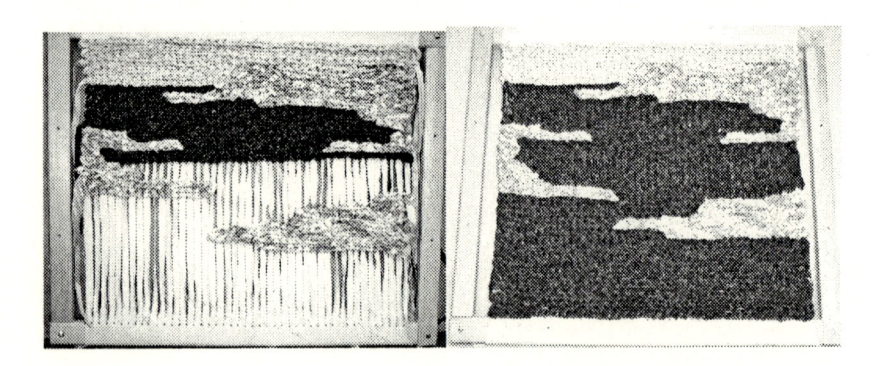

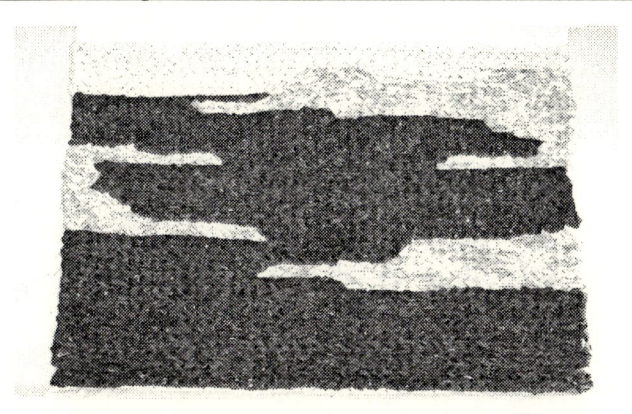

- When the rug surface is complete, remove the rug from the frame by pulling the staples or tacks out of the frame. Add additional rows to the rug surface if it is loose.
- Finishing is done by trimming the cloth backing to about two inches past the end of the warp slits. Use pinking shears for the trimming if you have them to minimize any fraying. Fold the edge to the back side of the rug, turn under a small hem and hand-sew it to the rug. The rug in the photo above is shown after removal from the frame and before hemming.

The Fine Points of the Cheater's Warp

There are a few considerations when using the cheater's warp, that affect rug construction. Because the warp strands have cut edges, and are narrow, they will fray. The cheaters warp, therefore, should not be subjected to abrasion by sliding stitches up and down the strands. The rug surface stitches need to be placed very close to their permanent position, and only moved a little bit as may be necessary to have closely spaced rows. The best way to avoid having to move stitches is to draw the rug design directly on the canvas or denim, *before the warp strands are cut.*

Do not pull or cut loose threads that develop between the warp strands. Instead, just work over them. When the rug is complete, any threads that have shown up at the surface can be clipped off.

The cheater's warp can also be used to make **round, oval and odd-shaped rugs**. After the base fabric is attached to the frame, draw on the outline of the rug shape. Follow the directions above to create the guidelines for cutting, but only cut the fabric inside the rug shape.

The rug surface and removal from the frame are completed as above, but turning the base fabric to the back will require easing to make it lay flat to the back of the rug to be hemmed. It is easiest to iron the backing fabric flat to the rug before hemming.

Using the Cheater's Warp with Light Fabrics on a Hanging Frame

With light fabrics the cheater's warp only works well on a hanging frame. This is also a nifty technique to weave a rug with a piece of calico that matches a quilt. You will need two dowels, at least ½-inch in diameter (larger is better) that are about three feet long. For your first rug with this method, use a piece of calico for the warp that is not more than 1½ yards long. The same fabric can be used for the rug surface as for the warp. The weaving fabric should be cut one-inch wide and folded in half, or 1½ inches wide and double-folded.

- The light fabric used for the warp will need to bunch up along the dowel to half its width, so a wide sleeve is sewn on both ends of the material. Fold over a two or three inch hem in each end of the fabric, and sew across with a sewing machine to create the sleeve.
- Then cut slits one inch apart along the length of the fabric, ending the slits about an inch from the hemming lines of the sleeves. (Discard the selvages if they contrast with the print.)
- Measure the width of the fabric. Divide the width by two. That will be the width of the finished rug. (For example, 44" fabric will make a 22" rug and 60" fabric will make a 30" rug.)
- Slide a dowel into one of the sleeves. Bunch up the fabric so that it is the proper width for the rug, and tape the edges to the dowel. Repeat with the second dowel at the other end of the fabric.
- Make a cord to hang the frame with a piece of heavy cord, twine or fabric strip. The cord should be about eight inches longer than the rug is wide. Tie the ends of the hanging cord to the dowel, just outside the gathered fabric. Use the cord to hang the frame up on a picture hanger, nail or screw. If you are short of room, use an over-the-door hanger, made for hanging up clothes.
- Make a second hanging cord the same way for the other end. This is the bottom end. If you are going to use the frame as a hanging frame, tie some weights to the cord or to the dowel itself. (A pair

of heavy boots makes a good weight, and the shoestrings can be used to tie the boots to the dowel or cord.)
- Alternately, you can pull the bottom of the rug away from the wall and hook the hanging cord to the back of a chair, or to a belt around your waist (similar to a back-strap loom).
- You can begin weaving anywhere on the warp, or use a non-tensioning method to cover the warp strands (or any combination). If you are weaving, try to keep the warp strands folded in half so that the print on the right side of the fabric shows.
- Note that in using light-weight fabric for the warp, you should never overfill the warp. The light fabric will tear along the slits.

A nice feature of the simple hanging frame is that you can work the most convenient end of the rug first, and then turn the frame over to work the other end. When the rug is completed, remove the dowels from the sleeve. Sew a piece of rug binding to the backing fabric about ¼ inch from the ends of the slits. Trim the backing fabric about one inch from the seam, and turn both the binding and the end of the fabric to the back of the rug. Sew the edge in place by hand.

You can make wider rugs, of course, using more than one piece of calico for the warp and longer dowels (or small boards) for the frame. If you do use different fabrics for the warp, make sure that they are of the same weight and weave, which will minimize any differences in how much the warp stretches.

CHAPTER 22
Scroll Frame Warps

Scroll frames are a specialized type of flat frame that allows you to create a rug that is twice as long as the frame itself. The name of the frame refers to two movable rollers at the ends, used to adjust the position of the working area of the warp. A great advantage in using a scroll frame is that the spacing of the warp strands is not fixed. The warp strands will slide along the rollers to accommodate the weight and bulk of the materials used for the rug surface. This makes them an excellent choice if you plan to use significantly lighter or heavier materials than are specified for any particular technique.

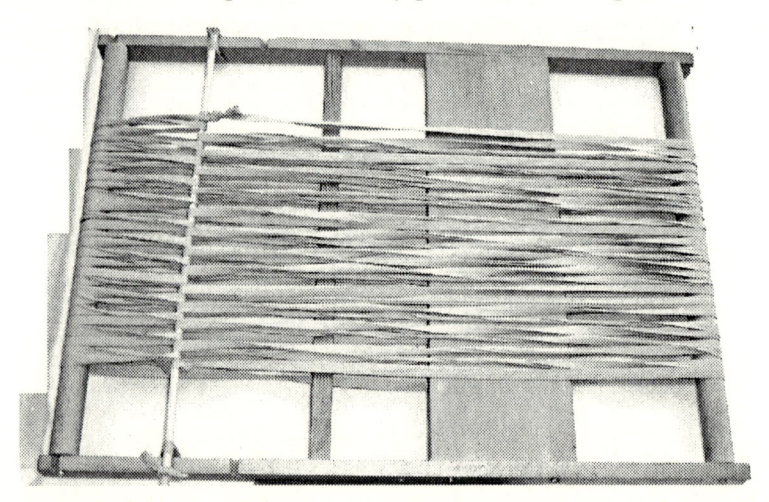

A typical scroll frame. The sides of the frame are secured with two central braces, permanently attached. The ends of the frame are two large dowels which are pinned so that they rotate freely.

Scroll Frame Warps

Because both of the warping patterns used on scroll frames are continuous warps, the frames really only work well with the non-tensioning techniques in Part I of the book. Any of those techniques will work in combination with each other, so an unlimited number of patterns, designs and textural variations are possible with a scroll frame.

One-way Continuous Warp

This warp is the easiest to put on a scroll frame and is used for rugs where fringes are desired at the ends. The material for the warp is wound onto the frame in one direction.

- Tie one end of the warp strand to a roller at the end of the scroll frame.
- Wind the warp around and around the frame until you have the desired number of warp strands in place.
- Safety pin (or tie) the end of the warp strand to the previous warp strand.
- Untie the beginning of the warp, and also pin (or tie) it to the next warp strand. The two pins should line up across from each other.
- Insert two guide bars into the warp, weaving them over and under several strands at a time, alternating between the two bars. The guide bars can be small pieces of lath, dowels, or even strips of heavy cardboard. These bars are used, not to increase tension on the warp, but as a guide when you rotate the warp around the frame. Without the guide bars, there is a tendency for the warp strands to move more at one end than the other, giving the rug an angled end. At left is a scroll frame with a one-way continuous warp installed. Notice the two guidebars woven through the warp.

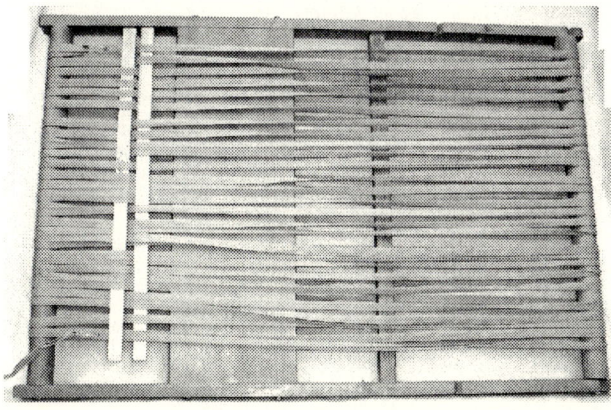

- Begin the rug surface just beyond the guide bars. When the work approaches the roller, and becomes awkward to handle, it is time to rotate the warp to the other side of the frame. Use the rollers at both ends and adjust the warp position if needed, using the guide bars as a reference point.
- Work the rug surface on the other side of the frame. When it approaches the other roller, again rotate the warp around the frame so that you can continue working.
- Stop working the rug surface when the beginning and end of the rug surface are still separated. The length of the fringed ends will be half of the distance separating the edges of the rug surface.
- The rug is cut off of the frame. Cut the warp strands in the middle of space between the beginning and end of the worked rug surface. Sew or tie the fringed ends to secure them. (Note: don't cut the rug off of the frame unless you also have time to do the finish work on the fringes.)

Reversing Continuous Warp

This warp is used for rugs with finished ends. It is a little more awkward to put on the frame, but is a lot easier to take off. To create this warp, you will need a ½-inch dowel that is a few inches longer than the frame is wide.

- Begin by tying the dowel to the frame, using heavy cord or fabric strip. The same knot is used as for the fifth stick frame, with the tie looped over the dowel, the ends passing under the frame and then the ends being tied on top of the dowel. Make sure that the dowel is straight across the frame.
- Tie one end of the warp directly to the dowel, leaving a tail about a foot long. Take the warp strand all of the way around the frame and back to the dowel.

Scroll Frame Warps 161

- Pass the warp under the dowel and reverse direction. Take the warp strand around the frame again coming back to the dowel.
- Pass the warp under the dowel again and go back the other way.

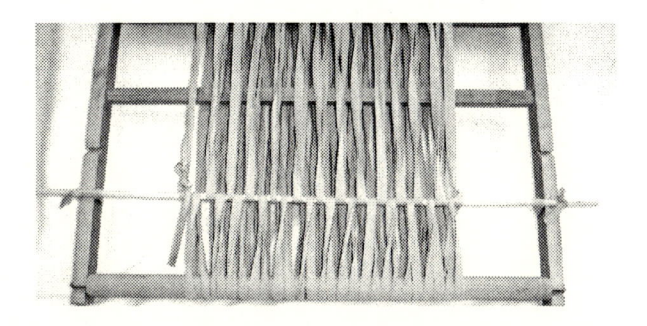

- The process is repeated until you have the desired number of warp strands on the dowel. Tie the end of the warp to the dowel itself, leaving a tail of a foot or so to lace back into the rug when it is finished.
- Begin working the rug surface on next to the dowel. It doesn't matter which side you start on. Don't untie the dowel from the frame just yet.
- When the rug surface is filled to the point that it approaches a roller, it is time to rotate the warp. Untie the dowel from the frame. Rotate the warp, using the rollers at both ends of the frame, until the worked area begins to appear on the other side of the roller.
- Then continue working the rug surface on the other side of the frame. When it approaches the other roller, rotate the warp again.
- Continue working the rug surface until you have it filled up to the dowel.
- To remove the rug from the frame, untie the warp ends from the dowel. Gently slide the dowel out of the loops of warp. It helps to twist the dowel back and forth during the process.
- Adjust the final rows of the rug surface stitching so that they fill in the warp loops left from the dowel removal. (See below.)
- Lace the two loose ends of the warp back into the rug surface.
- Let the rug lie flat to "relax" the warp.

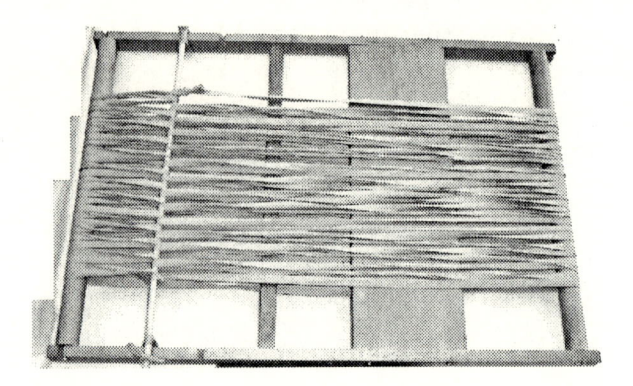

The non-tensioning methods used on this frame will slide along the warp. If you really pack in the rows of stitching near the dowels, the rows can simply be slid along the warp to fill the loops of warp that remain when the dowel is removed. If you find that you didn't quite add enough rows to accomplish that, slide several rows of stitches to the warp loops and add another row or two of stitching an inch or two away from the end of the rug. Don't try to work in the loops themselves since it isn't likely to give you a smooth edge.

If, once the rug is off of the frame, you find that you just didn't place your rows of stitching closely enough, you can fill in by sliding the stitches along the warp and adding more rows. See the techniques for inlaid designs in Chapter 8 for more ideas.

PART V: HANDBOOK

Tools Needed in Addition to a Frame

Lacing Needles. Other than the frame (which you can make yourself), there aren't many tools needed to make rugs. As you are getting started, you can use a large safety pin in place of a lacing needle, but if you plan on making a lot of rugs, a good steel lacing needle will save a lot of time. The best style for rug making is a six-inch, steel lacing needle with a broad, curved tip and blunt end (shown at the left side of the photo). The blunt end is important since it prevents the needle from catching and penetrating the fabrics used.

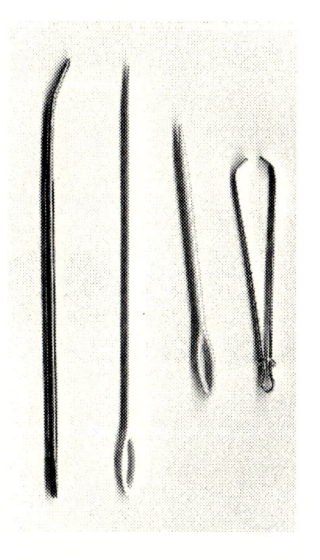

There are also plastic lacing needles that will work, but they need to have a large eye to handle fabric strips. Two sizes of plastic lacing needles are shown in the center of the photo. These are often sold as "bulky yarn" needles. Large sizes of tapestry needles will also work. For working with bulky fabrics a "pinch" style bodkin is useful to have. An example is shown at the right edge of the photograph.

Heavy fabrics can also be handled by attaching a large safety pin to the end of a strip.

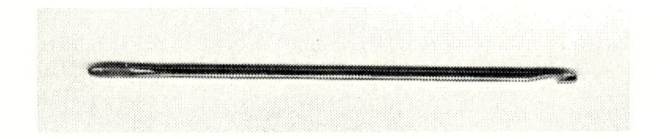

The only type of rug that really requires a specialized tool is the locker hooked rugs. Locker hooks (shown above) have a crochet hook at one end and an eye at the other. These hooks are not widely available in stores, so you may need to search for them on the internet.

Cutting Tools. If you like the look and feel of torn fabric strips for your rugs, all you need is a pair of sharp sewing scissors. However, if you want to make the more professional-looking rugs with double-folded strip, you'll need equipment to cut a lot of strip efficiently. A rotary cutter and mat are the most flexible for that process. Get the largest size mat you can afford and a good clear plastic cutting guide to fit it. If you fold the fabric neatly into layers, you can cut a 5-yard strip of calico or 3-yard strip of a single knit in a single pass. Even a whole sheet can be cut at once if it is arranged carefully.

Basic Sewing Tools. For the rugs that use a continuous warp or weft, you will need to create long sections of fabric strip. A sewing machine is useful in joining fabric sections or strips, making the whole process much faster than hand sewing.

Folding Tools. If you decide to make rugs as a business or to enter in a fair or contest, you'll want to double-fold any cotton strips. This process is made much easier with a pair of bias tape folders used in sequence. The folders need to be of the style that has a flat profile, such as the "Clover" brand. For fabric strip cut 1½ inches wide, you'll need one folder 25 mm size (1 inch) and a second folder 12 mm size (½ inch). The use of the folders is illustrated in the section on fabric preparation.

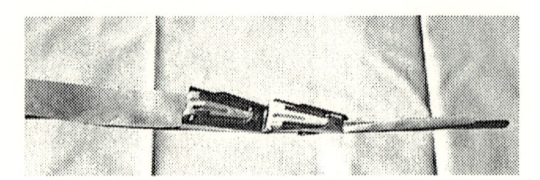

Tips for Handling Large Frames

A chronic problem for rug makers is that they just don't have enough floor space to accommodate large frames, permanently set up. Frames with fixed supports or legs can take up a lot of room, but generally, such supports aren't really needed. A fairly large frame (up to about three feet wide) can be handled in your lap. Sit in a comfortable chair near a kitchen or dining room table. Place a pillow in your lap. Put the end of the frame on your lap and prop the other end on the table so that it is at a comfortable angle for working. If you have an office-type chair with arms, the frame can be propped on the arms instead of the pillow. You can also work sitting on a couch with the frame propped in your lap and the other end leaning on a card table or something similar. Propping a frame in your lap is the best approach for techniques that require you to turn the frame around.

If you want to store your work out of the way, a simple cord hanger is a good solution. Tie a cord or piece of fabric strip to two corners of the frame, and hang it on a wall. This approach also lets you admire your work in progress.

Hanging a frame on a wall can also create a working place if you plan the height of the hanger. Sit in a comfortable chair facing the wall where you want to hang the frame. Prop the frame in your lap (on a pillow if desired), and lay the frame against the wall at the angle you find most comfortable for working. Have someone measure the height of the hanging cord to place the nail or screw to hang it on. Install the frame on the wall. When you want to work on the rug, all you need to do is bring your chair to the working position, sit down and get busy.

Very large frames are harder to handle and generally work best with permanent supporting legs. If you want to work with a large frame and can't leave it always set up, the next best approach is to prop all four corners on the back of four chairs. Unfortunately few chairs have backs at a convenient height for rug work, so you'll likely need to get a stool with a seat height which will correspond to the height of the frame.

Fabric Selection and Preparation

Most of the rugs illustrated in this book are made using light woven cotton and cotton blend fabrics. These are the most adaptable to frame rugs and are widely available as new fabric, as mill ends and as recycled clothing or bedding.

Light Woven Cottons (Calico, Broadcloth, etc.) Selecting cottons for rug making can be confusing since some fabrics will appear quite differently as yardage than they do in a finished rug. Remember that a rug will usually be seen at a distance of several feet, so stand back from a fabric to note how it appears. With a little practice you'll recognize good prints for rug making, but here is a general guide as you get started:

- Solid colors will accent the texture of the rug surface;
- Small closely spaced prints, like tiny florals will blend to an overall impression of a single color;
- Large all-over prints (like tropical florals) will give a general impression of tone (bright, dark, etc.) rather than of a particular color;
- Large widely spaced prints will create a speckled appearance in the rug;
- Watercolor prints will created a blended impression of tone and color;
- Plaids will disguise the texture of the rug surface and give only a general impression of color.

Rug making is a way to solve those fabric mistakes that happen sometimes, since even large garish prints or designs will disappear in the rug, leaving only a general impression of the colors of the fabric in the finished rug.

Be warned, however, that if you're one of those people who take up rug making with the idea of finally using up that huge fabric "stash," that it has never happened yet. Once you start working with rugs, you'll be even more susceptible to the sale table at the fabric store. The prints that wouldn't have gotten a second glance before—no matter how cheap they were—are now going to be awfully tempting. You'll be able to see that the stuff that would be terrible for sewing would be just perfect for a rug.

Woven cotton fabrics can be torn or cut into strips for rug making. Tearing strips from light cottons is the quickest method by far. Pre-wash new fabrics before tearing to remove any sizing and soften the fabric. Rugs made with torn strips have a more informal appearance than those made with cut and double-folded strip, but the time saved in preparation may be important if you are making rugs for use around the house. Some people even prefer the look of torn strips as more old-fashioned or softer. This is purely a personal choice.

Single-knit Fabrics. Single-knit fabrics can be used effectively in many of the frame-made rugs for the rug surface. However, they should not be used for the rug warp, or for the weaving techniques since they will stretch. Most of these fabrics have a natural curl when they are cut into strips which makes the fabric preparation very easy and gives the rug a finished look.

When using knit fabrics, always test for the direction of the "curl". Most T-shirt fabrics are can be cut along the length of the goods (parallel to the selvage) or across the width of the fabric. Interestingly, the direction of cutting determines which side of the fabric will show when it curls up. Usually, knits cut width-wise will show the back of the fabric and knits cut lengthwise will show the front side. Cut a short test strip one inch wide. Stretch it gently to see if the edges will curl under and which side of the fabric shows. If it creates the effect you want, go ahead and cut all of your strips that way. If it doesn't, cut the other direction.

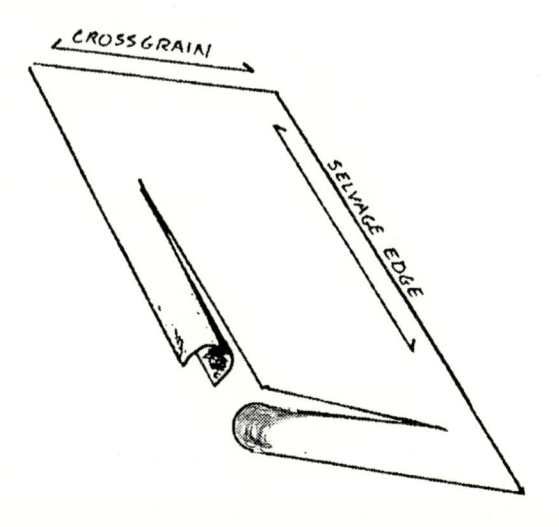

To make a single knit fabric strip curl up permanently, it needs to be stretched. A one-inch strip of knit fabric should be stretched to about 150% of its original length. For example, a two-foot section of strip should stretch to about three feet long. Don't overstretch knitted fabrics or the structure of the fabric itself will be weakened. Note that wider strips will stretch less and narrower strips will stretch more.

Occasionally single knits will only curl in one direction, so do a test cut both ways. (Some knit fabrics are heavily sized when they are new and may not curl at all until they are washed. If it won't curl at all, it is handled like a double-knit.)

Single knits can be cut as individual strips with scissors or a rotary cutter—don't try to tear knits. If you have cut the strips individually, join them end to end sewing the bias joint at right angles so that the seams are hidden. That will give the smoothest appearance in the rug. After they are stitched together, pull on the fabric strip firmly to make the strip curl up and hide the raw edges. If you have an ultra-modern décor, look for single knits with a shiny or metallic finish since they make extraordinarily eye-catching rugs.

Heavier and Lighter Knit Fabrics. Some sweatshirt knits, velours and velveteens will also curl, and will make for interesting rug surfaces. Do not use these fabrics for warp, only for rug surfaces. Very light knits can also be used—for example some sheer drapery fabrics. These light fabrics can be surprisingly durable in a rug, but don't plan to use them in a high traffic area since they will skid around and bunch up. Ideally they should be used only over a carpet.

Double-knit fabrics don't curl naturally and have to be handled like woven fabrics. The strips are cut individually and joined with the overlapping bias joint. In general double-knits should be cut one inch wide, but the heavier ones (and textured ones) work best at ¾ inches or even ½ inch.

The vintage polyester double-knits are often extremely durable and fade resistant so they do have their adherents. Other folks swear by rugs made with double-knits since they finally have something they can do just to use up the stuff, or recycle old clothing.

Wool Fabrics. Wool fabric makes an extraordinary rug, but is not suitable for all of the frame rug methods. Use wool for twisted warps on a straight frame, wagon wheel rugs or straight weaving on a flat frame. The best-looking wool rugs will use pre-folded strips to hide the raw edges, but these fabrics are too heavy to use with bias tape folders. Instead, the old pin-and-soak method is the most efficient.

When I first came across this technique, I didn't really believe that it would work, but it does quite well. Cut heavy wool strips 1½ or 2 inches wide. Fold the edges to the center, then fold the strip in half to create the double-fold. Pin the folds in place with straight pins. Drop the pinned strip into cold water and let it get completely saturated. Note that woolens that have a lot of lanolin in them will want to float, so you'll have to push then under the water. I usually leave the strips in the cold water about 15 minutes to make sure that they get completely wetted. Pull the strip out of the water and hang it to completely dry. Once dry, the folds are set—but they aren't "permanent." If you aren't going to use the strip immediately, you can remove the pins and roll the strips into balls, making sure not to unfold the strip as you roll it.

Another source of wool for frame made rugs is old wool braided rugs. There are a lot of older rugs that may be coming apart at the rounds, or are just too large, or have a damaged spot that would be difficult to repair. These rugs can be salvaged and the wool recycled for frame rugs. Take the rug apart at the sewing or lacings between the rounds. Cut the braids into a convenient length (three or four yards long) and secure the ends with rubber bands. Most old rugs also need a good wash, so wash the braids in warm water with a mild soap in the bathtub. Rinse well and let dry. The braids are then unraveled to use for frame rugs.

Novelty Fabrics. Specialty fabrics can be used to achieve dramatic effects in frame rugs. Metallics, silks, linens, and such work well for rug surfaces and in wall hangings. Don't be afraid to experiment. The only practical consideration when using specialty fabrics is washability. If the rug will be subject to heavy soil, make sure to test wash all fabrics before using them. Shiny fabrics should be double-folded to accent their appearance. As a general rule, woven novelty fabrics can be handled like woven cottons, and knitted novelties like cotton knit fabric. To estimate the fabric consumption for novelty fabrics, find a fabric above that is of about the same weight.

Denim, Canvas and Other Heavy Cotton Fabrics. Heavy cotton fabrics can be used for frame rugs, especially the ones woven on flat frames. They should be cut four to six inches wide and double-folded or triple-folded for use. These fabrics will need to be ironed to set the folds. Another way to handle heavy cottons is to roll the strips into a tube as you attach them to the flat frame for weaving.

Estimating Fabric Consumption

At last count, there were directions in this book for almost 40 basic rug construction methods. With all of the various materials that can be used in any of them, it becomes a virtual impossibility to give exact yardage figures for every potential combination. The general guidelines below will help you to estimate the fabric requirements for your rug. These yardage numbers are based on using the same materials specified in the instructions—which for most techniques is 1½ inch strips of cotton or blend fabrics with a weight of about four ounces, which includes most clothing fabrics and sheet goods.

For **flat profile rugs** such as the darned rugs on the pegged frame and the straight weaving on the flat frame, allow one yard of 44" cotton or blend fabric for each square foot of the rug.

For **light weight rugs**, such as the darned rugs, allow 1½ yards of 44" cotton or blend fabric for each square foot. .

For **medium weight rugs**, such as the Amish Knot, Bess Chet and Twined rugs, allow two yards of 44" cotton or cotton blend fabrics for each square foot of the rug.

For **raised pile rugs**, such as the Flat Wrap, modified Hooked and Rya Knot, allow four yards of 44" cotton fabric if the rug has a two-inch pile height. For each additional inch of pile height, add another yard for each square foot of the rug.

If you are using heavier fabrics, the fabric consumption will be less, and lighter fabrics will require more yardage. To determine an exact yardage requirement for a particular rug type with a particular fabric, you will need to do a test piece. First, weigh the fabric you are going to be using and calculate how much one yard weighs. For example if you have a piece of fabric that is 60 inches wide, and 2½ yards long, that weighs 20 ounces, each yard weighs 8 ounces (20 divided by 2½ equals 8). Make a test rug using a frame that is one square foot for the easiest calculation. Weigh the test rug. If the rug is one square foot and weighs 8 ounces (as in the example above) the rug requires one yard of fabric for each square foot.

Tearing vs. Cutting Fabrics

Woven cotton fabrics can be cut or torn to make strips for rugs. If you do not want to fold the strip for your rug, it is best to tear the fabric into strips after pre-washing it to remove the sizing. (Old clothing has already been washed, so it is ready to tear.) Just clip the edge of the fabric an inch or two down and hold the two sections apart and pull. The fabric should tear along a straight thread. After tearing remove any loose threads that cling to the strip.

Many fabrics are either too worn to use for rugs or too loosely woven to tear. In the photo on this page, look at the bottom fabric example. Notice how the edges are very loose and the fabric itself has fractured. If a torn strip has this appearance, the fabric is too loosely woven to be torn into strips for rugs. These fabrics can still be used for rugs, but the strips must be cut instead.

Some "homespun" and tattersall types of fabrics are woven with a heavier cotton thread and some of them will tear and fold themselves if they are handled just right, as shown in the photograph on this page. Prewash the fabric. Make a tear for the first rug strip and if the edge of the strip wants to turn over, you're in luck. Make the next tear from the opposite end of the fabric to get the edges turning over to the same side. Finish tearing the strip alternating the end of the fabric from which the strip is torn each time.

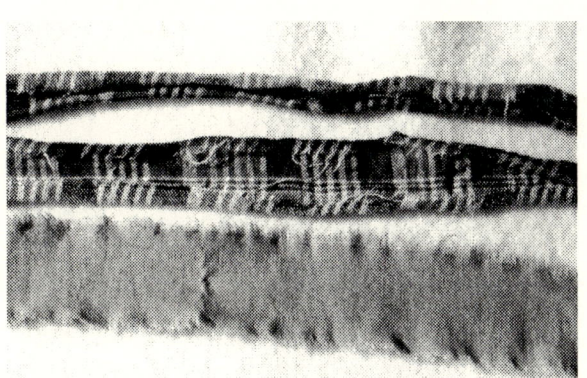

If you want to double-fold woven cotton fabric strip, the fabric should not be pre-washed before cutting since a little sizing helps the strip glide more smoothly through the folders. Strip should always be cut (not torn) if it is going to be folded.

Never cut light cotton fabrics on the bias (diagonal) for use in rug making. Bias-cut strips will stretch—even after the rug is completed—loosening the rug structure. The only time bias-cut strips are appropriate is when a shaggy surface is created, and the knotted materials aren't an integral part of the rug structure.

Cotton knit fabrics have to be cut since they won't tear cleanly. Before cutting, test for the direction of the curl in the fabric. Usually with single-knit fabrics, a lengthwise cut will curl up into a tube which shows the "right side" of the fabric, and cutting along the width will show the "wrong side" or back of the fabric. If you want to use T-shirts for rugs and have the "right side" show, cut the shirt lengthwise (from hem to shoulder) and then join the strips using the regular bias joint. That will hide the seams in the finished strip when it curls up.

Heavy fabrics such as corduroy or wool may or may not tear cleanly, so you just have to test a strip of a particular fabric to find out. These types of fabrics really generate a lot of lint when torn, so it is best to do that outdoors.

Joining Fabric Strips for Rug Making

When you have all of your strip cut, you're ready to join them into a continuous length for rug making. Match the type of strip that you want to use with the joining method. Unfolded strips should be joined using the overlapping bias joint and folded strips should be joined using the regular bias joint.

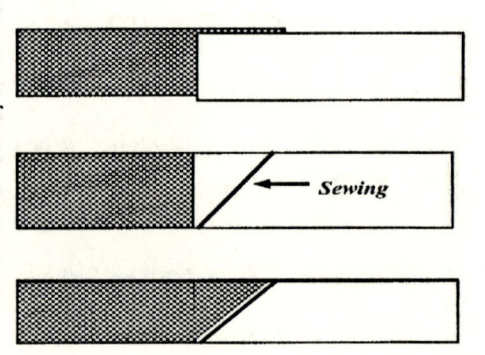

The Overlapping Bias Joint. Use this joining with unfolded strips. The diagonal seam will spread the bulk of the fabric out so that it doesn't form a bump in the rug. The ends of the two strips are overlapped in a straight line. The overlap should be about the same as the width of the strips themselves. A seam is sewn on the diagonal across the two strips. The corners which extend beyond the diagonal seam are clipped off, leaving about a ¼-inch seam allowance.

The Regular Bias Joint. This joining is used with strip that will be folded or curled into a tube. In sewing this joint the "right sides" of the fabric are placed together at right angles. A diagonal seam is sewn across the corner, and then clipped to a ¼-inch seam allowance. Notice that the seam is on the "wrong side" of the fabric. When the strips are straightened out, the seam should appear to run diagonally across the strip (spreading out the bulk).

Cutting line

Sewing line

When the strip is folded (woven cottons) or curled (single-knit fabrics), the seam is hidden within the strip and is nearly invisible in the finished rug.

No-Sew Ways to Add Strip or Change Colors. Any of the frame rugs which use short strips in the rug surface allow for color changes to be made fairly easily by just working a six- or eight-inch tail back into the stitches forming the surface. For the rugs which use a long, continuous strip (like the Bess Chet), it is useful to know how to add strip or change colors of strip when a sewing machine isn't handy. There are at least eight different slit-and-loop methods of splicing fabric strip, but there is only one—the bow tie joint—that doesn't result in a noticeably thick and lumpy knot, so that is the only one I recommend for making rugs. The bow tie joint is not as efficient as the joints made on sewing machines, but it can be done anywhere using just a small pair of scissors.

Cut or tear cotton fabric strips one to 1½ inches wide—choose one width for the entire rug. You'll want the strips to be as long as you can get from the piece of fabric that you are using.

At both ends of each strip clip a tiny slit one inch or a little more from the end. The slit should be as small as possible—just large enough for another strip to pass through. Because the slit should be small a pair of embroidery scissors or thread nippers is a good tool to use. Make sure that the end of the slit is at least an inch from the end of the fabric strip.

Insert the end of the first strip into the slit in the second strip. Then insert the end of the second strip through the slit in the first strip.

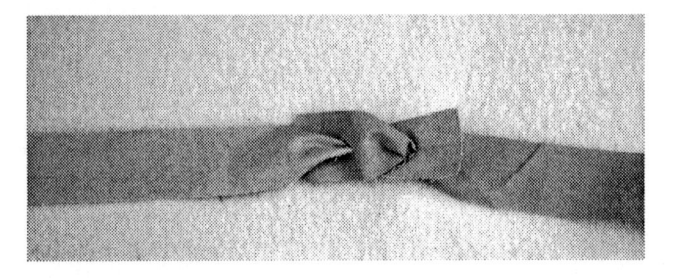

Pull gently to tighten the knot and adjust the strip ends so that they lay flat and curl around the strip forming a bow tie sort of shape. In making the rug, try to keep these ends laying flat against the strip. If you find that a corner sticks up anyway it can be clipped off—but only if it is a corner. If the whole end sticks up for some reason, it will need to be tucked back into the rug surface.

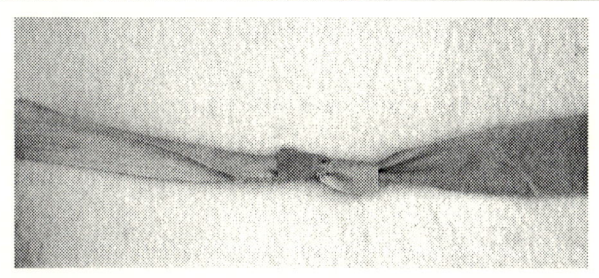

Spinning Warp or Weft Strips

A question I am often asked by rag rug weavers using a regular looms is how to handle the fabric strip so that it is less "thready." The edge threads can work up to the surface with any strip that isn't double-folded and it doesn't matter whether the strip was cut or torn. The more that a strip is subject to abrasion, the more threads will work loose from the edge.

There is an easy way to minimize threadiness, and it also works as a second-best choice if you don't want to double-fold the fabric strip for a continuous warp. Cut or tear the fabric strip, and sew it to a continuous length using the overlapping bias joint. Then wind the strip onto a small dowel or spindle. Pull the fabric strip off one end of the dowel—not allowing the dowel to rotate. You will notice that the strip is twisted which will hold in edge threads. This procedure is actually a primitive form of spinning and can be used with any type of fabric strip. Roll the twisted strip into a ball as soon as it comes off of the dowel.

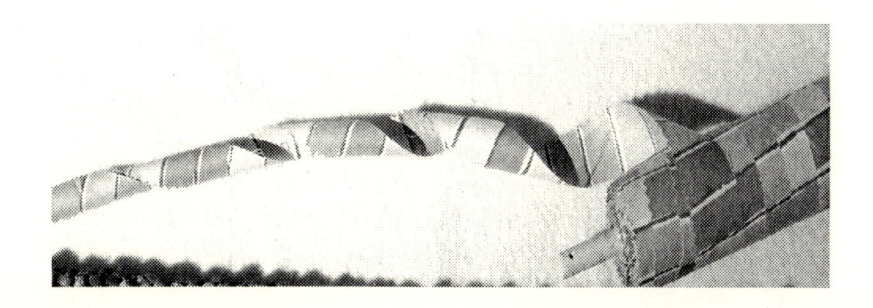

For even more twists in the strip, you can roll the strip onto a second dowel as it is pulled from the first one. The strip is then pulled off the end of the second dowel. Be cautious in removing the strip from the second dowel though, since if you pull it off one end, more twists will be added, but if you pull it off the other end, it will untwist.

Double-folding Warp and Weft Strips

If you want to make professional-looking rugs with woven cotton fabrics, you need to know how to double-fold the strips to hide the raw edges. Particularly if you are intending to sell your rugs, using folded strips will give you the greatest return for your time. The strip for some older rugs was ironed by hand which is quite time-consuming, but it does work. You'll be able to fold strip much more efficiently using a pair of bias tape folders.

Do not pre-wash fabrics that you plan to double-fold. For light cottons cut the fabric strip 1½ inches wide on the straight on the grain of the fabric (parallel to the selvage). Do not include the selvage in the cut strips since it has a different weight than the rest of the fabric. Never cut woven light cottons on the bias (diagonal) since the strip will continue to stretch even after the rug is made and the rug won't hold its shape well.

Cut the strips using scissors or a rotary cutter and mat. Then sew the strips into one continuous length using the regular "bias joint" (see illustration). Make sure that all of the seams are going the same direction. With print fabrics, it is easy to sew the right sides together, but solid color fabrics are a different story and you have to watch the seams carefully.

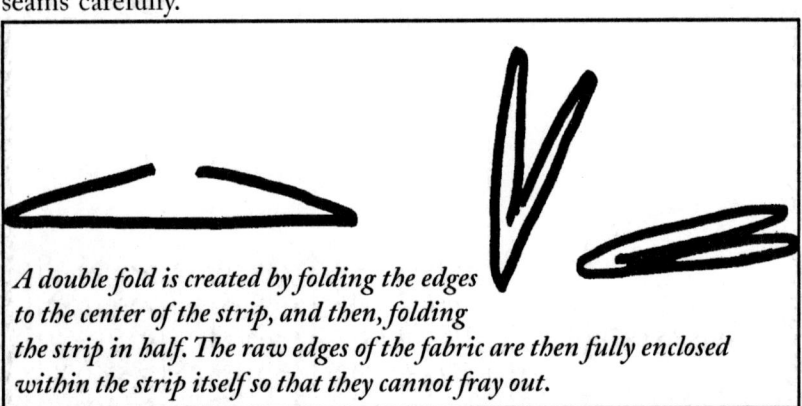

A double fold is created by folding the edges to the center of the strip, and then, folding the strip in half. The raw edges of the fabric are then fully enclosed within the strip itself so that they cannot fray out.

The old fashioned-way of double-folding was simply to fold the edges under and then fold the strip in half and iron it by hand. I've seen yards and yards of this rug strip carefully put away for decades and it always amazes me how much labor must have gone into a rug with fabrics prepared this way.

When I first began rug making, I wasn't much more efficient. I would double-fold the fabric strip by hand and roll it into a tight ball. I'd discovered that you really didn't need to iron cotton strips since just heat would set the folds. So the hand-rolled balls went into the oven set on "Warm" for a couple of hours. This really only worked well with cotton and blends that were at least 70% cotton.

I knew there had to be a better way and by experimentation found that two bias tape folders used in sequence would double-fold fabric strip. These only work when the strip to be folded is fed perfectly straight through the folders. If you have a good friend or patient spouse or child, they can handle the feeding operation while you pull the strip through the folders and iron it or roll it up tightly. That works for a little while until your helper goes on strike.

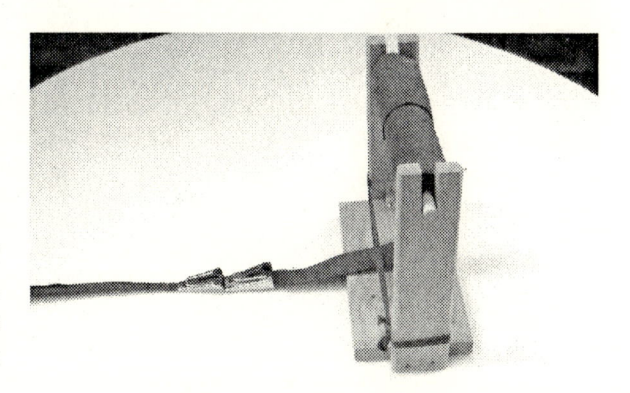

Most of the time a rug maker will need to be able to handle the folding operation single-handedly which means you'll need some modest equipment. As you are starting, the easiest set up is to use a paper towel tube. As you sew the strips together wind them flat (no twists) onto the cardboard tube. When the strips are all rolled up, you'll need a spindle to put the tube onto. In a pinch, a broomstick handle will fit through the tube—just prop the ends of the broom between two kitchen chairs. The roll can be several feet from where you set up the folders. If you think you're going to be doing a lot of rug making, it is worth the time to make yourself a simple wooden stand like the one shown in the illustration. The uprights are cut out to hold a dowel, and the fabric strip can be rolled directly onto the dowel as shown or the dowel can hold a paper towel tube with the fabric strip on it. Just be sure not to twist the strip as you roll it onto the dowel or tube.

Next you'll need to secure the folders so that they don't move. If you're going to iron the strip as it comes out of the folders, this can be done with large safety pins set into an old ironing board cover. A more practical solution is to make a permanent folder-holder on a small piece of wood or paneling. Use a heavy fabric (like a scrap of denim) cut and inch or two wide. Place the smallest folder in position on the board, lay the denim strip across it and thumbtack it to the board (or use a staple gun). The fabric sleeve should be tight enough to keep the folder from moving, and solidly connected to the board so that it won't work loose as you pull the strip through the folders. Then set the larger folder in place and make a sleeve for it just the same way. Don't try to use a single sleeve for both folders since you'll need to be able to remove the folders individually in case of a jam. Your folding board can then be clamped to the ironing board. If you are just going to roll the strip into balls, the board can be clamped to a tabletop or other convenient spot.

An even more permanent folding rig can be made using a single board or piece of plywood to hold both the stand for the fabric strip and the two folders. Elaborations include adding handles and guides.

Feed the strip from the roll straight through the folders *wrong side up* so that the seam allowances will be hidden within the folded strip. Then pull a length of strip through the folders and iron it or roll it up. If you feel like more tension is needed, set a heavy book or two on top of the strip just before it enters the folders. (For years, I used an old flat iron as a weight to add tension to the fabric strip as it was pulled through the folders.)

Of course, over the years I've designed and built more and more elaborate folding apparatuses and each was at least some improvement in efficiency over the previous models. But the use of two bias tape folders together is still the basis for double-folding. There are all sorts of possibilities if you want to get creative, but complicated folding machinery isn't really necessary even if you plan to go into the rug-making business.

Triple-folding Strips for Flat Profile Rugs

For the rugs which use wide flat strips, such as the straight weaving on flat frames and frame braid rugs, heavy fabrics can be just double-folded, but lighter weight fabrics must be triple-folded to give them enough body for a rug. A triple-fold creates a strip that is six layers thick so that even very light cottons will have enough bulk for a rug.

Because of the folding pattern, triple-folded strip is usually ironed to set the folds before rug-making.

To make a triple-fold, first fold the strip itself in half lengthwise. Then fold the raw edges over for about one-third of the width of the strip. Finally, the first folded edge is folded again so that it covers the raw edges.

You can cut the fabric strips to length for the rug before you triple-fold each one, or do that after the rug itself is finished. Once the folds are ironed-in, the strip needs to be stored carefully so that the folds set properly (and don't unfold themselves before you can use them). As soon as possible after ironing, lay the strips flat against each other and slip a light rubber band around the bundle to hold them together. I usually rubber-band a single color together, then use cloth strips to stabilize several bundles as shown below.

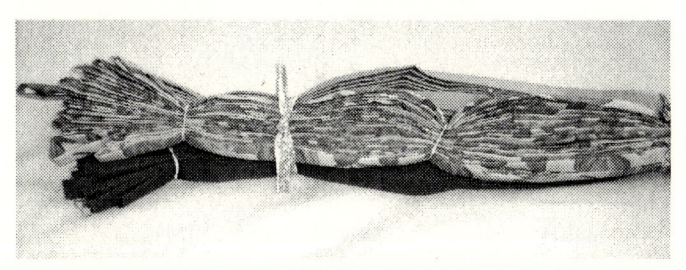

Using Alternate Materials for Rugs

The strongest, most durable rugs will be the ones made using fabric for the warp—especially the rugs in Part I which use the continuous warp. I know, however, that most people who want to make rugs for fun are not going to want to double-fold fabric strip for their rugs: "Isn't there something else that I can buy already made?"

You may be tempted to buy double-folded bias tape at the sewing store, but don't use that as a substitute. Bias tape stretches and the rug won't hold its shape. Instead, use the soft nylon cord, which is sold at hardware stores and sporting goods stores. That cord has a knitted nylon sheath over a synthetic core and is a little less than a quarter of an inch in diameter. It is usually sold as "utility" cord for tying down tents and tarps, but it works fine for the continuous warp on pegged frames. It also has a slick enough surface to allow the stitches to slide easily, making it a good choice for a freeform rug as well. You can use the nylon cord for all of the techniques in Part I, except the knotted shags since the knots won't hold. Nylon cord will fray when it is cut, so the ends need to be heat sealed (pass the end through the flame of a candle just long enough to melt some of the fibers—not making it actually catch on fire).

For the knotted shags, you can use a very heavy cotton cording, which is sold for macrame work, and is a little less than ¼-inch in diameter. The synthetic macrame cord usually has too many ridges to work well as a warp. Don't use lighter cotton cording since it will stretch when your rug is off the frame.

On frame made rugs, the warp material must be balanced with the rug surface material. For example, the Amish knot rugs are shown using 1½-inch cotton strip for both the warp and the rug surface. If you switch to a thin cord for the warp, the stitches will not have enough bulk to fill between the warp strands, and the rug will pull in. To balance a thinner warp, the strips for the rug surface will need to be cut wider (about two inches), or the pegs on the frame placed more closely together.

If you want to use a thin cord for the warp of a rug, the best choice is to use the continuous warp on the scroll frame (shown later in the Handbook section). That warp pattern will automatically adjust itself to the bulk of the rug surface material.

I'm certain that many people will want to adapt these techniques for use with yarn, instead of fabric strip. Yarns will work with many of the techniques shown for the rug surface, but should *never* be used for the warp of a rug—it just isn't strong enough. The best choice is to use a fabric warp (or nylon cord) for the warp, and use the yarns for the rug surface only. Bulky yarns have about half the mass of the fabric strips shown in the rug surfaces, so if you are using them for a pegged frame, use the ¼-inch warp spacing shown in the section on locker hooking. Of course, with yarns the continuous warp on the scroll frame is also a very good choice.

Wool yarn is the best choice for rug surfaces and combines well with a heavy linen cord (6-ply) used as the warp on a scroll frame. The 6-ply linen is sold for lacing braided rugs together. Yarns can also be used with the nylon cord as a warp. If you want to use a pegged frame, and lighter weight yarns, you can use several strands of yarn together as if they were a single strand.

Lacing Rug Sections Together

Any of the rugs made using a continuous warp will work in assembling a large rug from smaller blocks. The critical element with a large rug is its weight, and if you will be making one, use a fabric warp 1½ inches wide.

In assembling a large rug, arrange the individual blocks so that their warp strands are all going the same way. The blocks are laced together in rows in the same direction as the warp. If the rug is longer than it is wide, the warp strands should run the length of the rug. Once the rows of blocks are assembled, the rows are laced together to form the rug.

Lacing is done from the back side of the rug in rows of squares. For example if your rug will be three squares wide and four squares long, the first step in the assembly is to lace each row of four squares together in order.

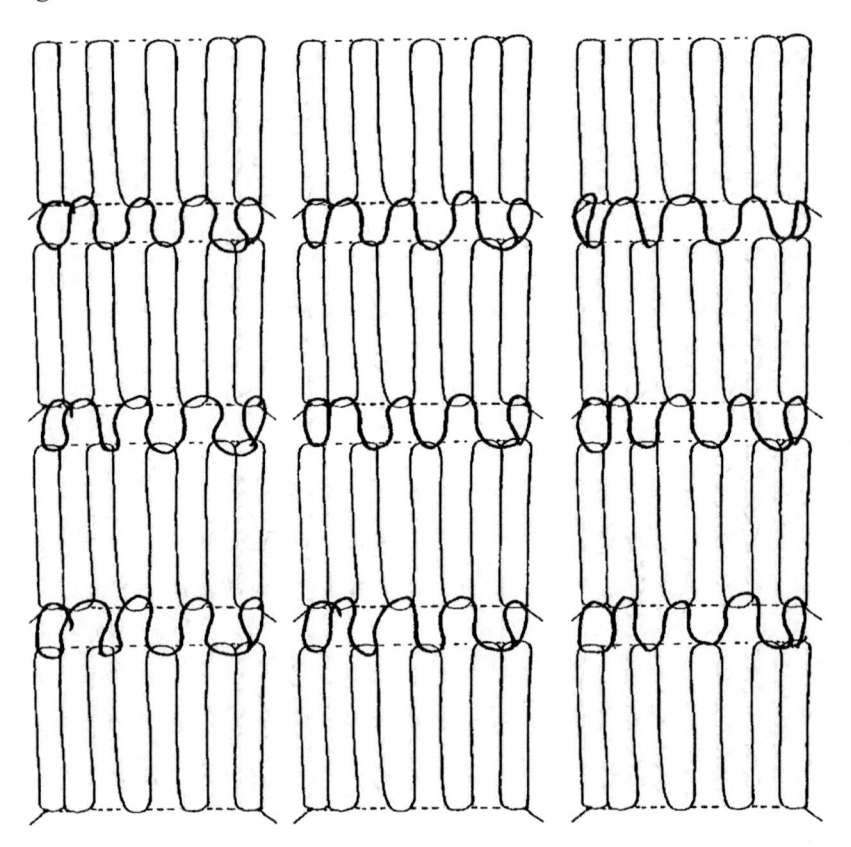

Pick up the first two squares to be joined and lay them face down on a table. Thread a large-eye lacing needle or tapestry needle with the fabric strip. These squares should have the end loops of the warps matched up. Insert the lacing needle in the first end loop of one square (going down) and then in the matching warp loop (coming back up). This forms one whip stitch with the fabric strip.

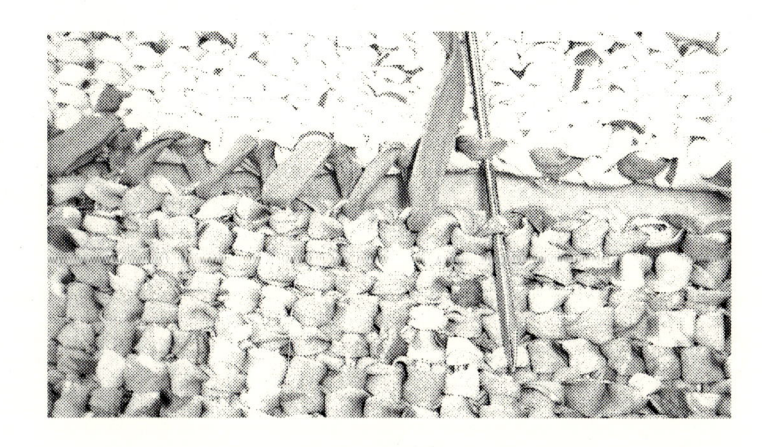

Pull the lacing strip through, leaving at least a six-inch tail. Repeat the stitch through the same two loops. Move to the next matching pair of warp loops and make one stitch. Work across to the other end making one whip stitch in each matching pair of warp loops and placing two stitches in the corner pair. Clip off the lacing strip leaving at least six inches of tail.

Pick up the next square in the row and repeat the process. All of the squares in the row are joined in the same manner. When one row of squares is laced together, repeat the process with each of the next rows until your rug pieces are all joined into rows.

To lace the rows of squares together, you will be working with the whip stitch again, but the stitches will be placed in the warp between rows of stitches. Note that those spaces won't be lining up neatly (they never do) so this lacing takes a little more finesse. Make two whip stitches in the corner and one whip stitch on the warp strands of the two pieces, matching them as closely as possible. Stitch along the two edges of the blocks, keeping them snugly together. When you reach the end of the first pair of blocks, there should be four corners which should line up. If they don't, go back and readjust the placement of the last few whip stitches. Where the four corners meet, place two whip stitches in the aligning corners. These stitches are worked in the loops of warp that form the corners.

Work down the row, matching all corners and placing two whip stitches at each corner. If you run out of lacing strip part way through, make a second stitch with it at that point, leaving at least a six-inch tail. Begin a new lacing strip—also with two stitches and leaving a tail.

When all of the rows of blocks are laced together, use the lacing needle to work the tail ends of the lacing strip into the rug. This is also done from the back side, but these tails should be threaded underneath a row of knots working up a nearby warp strand. If you are working with a fairly slippery fabric, sew the ends in place with needle and thread so that they can't work loose.

Using a "Pinned" Frame

Several of the more common frame designs were discussed earlier in the book, but there are many other types of frames that can be used for rug making. There isn't room to list each and every type, but the "pinned" frame is so easy to construct, that it just has to be included. The "pinned" frame, also known as a "slip" frame is composed of four round dowels and four right-angle plumbing fittings. The plumbing fittings are permanently glued to one end only of each of the dowels. The frame is assembled by fitting the "empty" ends of the dowels into the fittings to secure them. The only thing that holds this frame together is the warp itself.

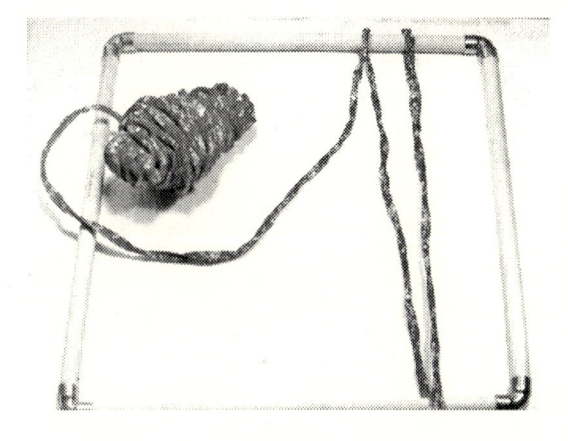

The warp is sewn into a loop around one dowel and then wound around the frame, usually in a figure-eight. Note that, like a scroll frame, the warp strands can slide along the frame to any spacing.

This makes the pinned frame very versatile for use with many different types and weights of materials in any of the non-tensioning techniques. Pinned frames can also be used for small woven projects, but only up to about 12 inches in any direction, since there isn't any good way to release the tension on the warp.

Another feature of the pinned frame is that it is easily adapted to a bi-directional warp for use with any of the rug making methods that require warp strands in two directions.

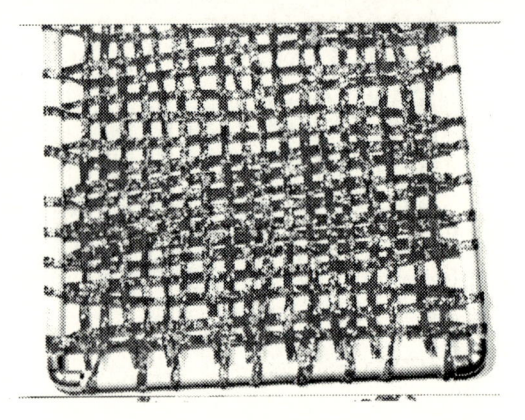

Removing a rug from a pinned frame is also quite simple since it is only a matter of slipping the dowels out of the warp loops. (That's why it is also called a "slip" frame.) However, once removed from the frame, the rug will have loops around the sides. The non-tensioning techniques can be worked through these loops to form a border, or the loops can be chained (like a crochet chain) to create an edge.

Alternately, since the warp is a continuous warp, the slack can be pulled through the worked areas as in the freeform shaping technique discussed in Chapter 8.

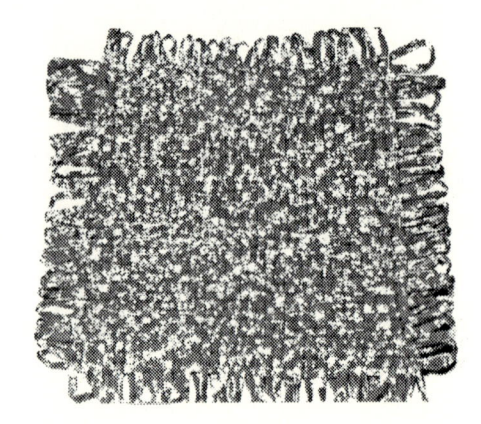

A Miscellany About Frames

Over the years I've built many, many frames of various types and sizes, ending up with quite a collection of them. There are a few things that make some frames more practical than others.

About twenty years ago, I'd gotten bored with small frames and decided to make myself a large one. Essentially, it was a stripped-down loom designed for cloth warp and was tall enough that I could stand while working, which I like to do. Just over four feet wide, the frame let me make large rugs in a single piece. In an attempt at practicality, I'd designed it to fold up for storage, but in spite of that the frame still took up too much space. After about three years, I finally took it down and haven't used it since. I found that a scroll frame with a reversing warp would accomodate rugs of the same size without being such a space hog.

When we had the rug shops, I found myself making the same sizes of rugs over and over again. This was particularly so with the rugs made with straight weaving on wrapped frames. That situation made it efficient to have several standard sizes of frames available, already wrapped and ready to go. The square and rectangular frames did double-duty with round and oval wagon wheel rugs too.

These frames were "permanent" and required a method to store them efficiently when not in use. I found that a metal shelf-bracket, placed high on the wall worked very well to keep them handy without taking up precious floor or shelf space.

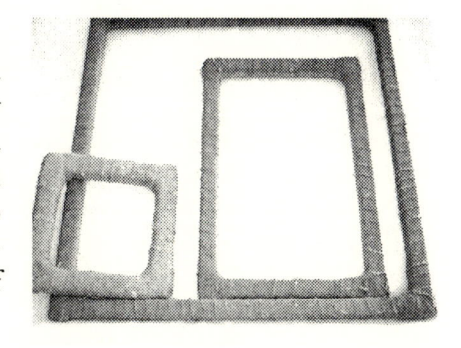

On the other hand, managing regular flat frames and pegged frames became quite a challenge. There were so many sizes of rugs and some required pegs on all sides, some with pegs only on two sides and some with no pegs at all. In order to not be completely overrun with various fixed frames, I adopted a system using pairs of interchangeable, lap-jointed segments.

These were made up in different lengths from 18 inches to 48 inches (in pairs). Some were plain and some had pegs at one-inch spacing. With that system, it was reasonably easy to put together the required frame by just selecting the proper components and using wing nuts to hold them together.

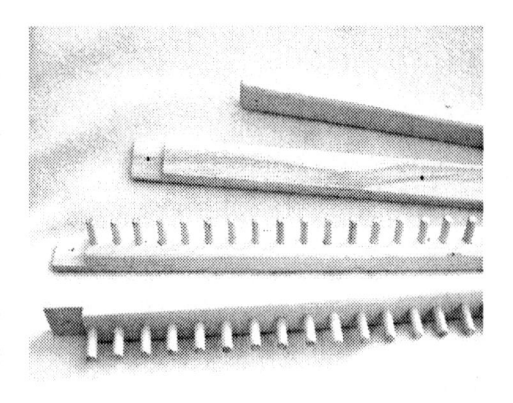

If you find yourself in the business of making frame-based rugs, I'd strongly suggest adopting a similar system. Having the frame segments built takes an investment of course, but it saves a tremendous amount of time in the long run.

The most interesting frame I ever saw wasn't a frame at all. It was only a series of pegs inserted into the logs of an old barn. The rugmaker's son was not sure of the method that his mother had used to make the rugs, only that she had strung some sort of warp (baling twine sometimes, he thought) and worked rag strips over the warp to make the rugs. Since there were two rows of pegs, separated by about four feet, I'd suppose she had used one of the non-tensioning methods. Whatever type of rugs she'd made will remain a mystery, but the pegs on the barn wall were a poignant reminder of the frugality of rural living in the early twentieth century.

Caring for Frame Rugs

How to care for a rug depends entirely on the materials used in its construction. If you used washable materials, the rug will be washable. For rugs with a shaggy surface, the washing has to be done by hand, however. Rugs with a smooth and tight surface, not more than 36 inches across can generally be machine washed—if you make them from washable fabrics. (Use the gentle cycle, a mild detergent and no bleach.) Washing is usually not required more than once every few months for rugs that receive basic care. The rugs should be shaken out regularly and vacuumed *on both sides* using the suction-only attachment (usually labeled the upholstery tool).

Larger rugs, those with shaggy surfaces, and ones made with wool can be hand washed in the bathtub. Fill the tub with warm water and a mild soap. Let the rug soak long enough to become saturated. Hand agitate and squeeze the soapy water through the rug. Push the rug to the end away from the drain and let the water out. When water stops running out of the rug, refill the tub with warm water and agitate again. Drain the tub. Repeat the rinsing as needed until all of the soapy water is out of the rug. Preliminary drying of the rug is by laying it between two towels and compressing it by walking on it or rolling it up in the towels.

To clean rugs that are too large for a washing machine or bathtub, a carpet cleaning machine is recommended. Machines which spray water on the rug, and then suck it out are the best. Never use a machine with rotating brushes. Always clean both sides of the rug. Do not use the aerosol spray rug cleaners on rugs. They can damage the fabrics and often the residue remaining on the rug actually attracts dirt.

Rugs should not be dried in the dryer since they become too heavy when wet for most home machines. Instead, lay the damp rug flat to dry, out of direct sunlight. Large rugs may be draped over a clothesline, railing or banister for preliminary drying, but when they are still slightly damp, they should be laid flat to finish. Shape the rug if necessary for the last part of its drying.

If you plan to store your rug for any length of time, roll it up with its "best" side in. Store it in a dry location, out of direct sunlight. Rugs can be wrapped in a sheet to keep them clean in storage, but don't use plastic bags, since that can encourage mildew. To freshen a rug that has been in storage (if needed), sprinkle it with baking soda and let it set for several hours. Vacuum the baking soda off before using.

Key to the Rugs on the Covers

Front cover, upper photo:
Center: Wagon wheel rug, Chapter 16

Clockwise from upper left:
Straight weaving on a flat frame, Chapter 14
Twill, Chapter 13
Bess Chet, Chapter 5
Woven on pegged frame, Chapter 13

Front cover, lower photo:
Top row, left to right:
Knotted shag, Chapter 2
Darned, Chapter 3
Amish knot, Chapter 4

Center row, left to right:
Bess chet, Chapter 5
Combination, Chapter 8
Raised bess chet, Chapter 5

Bottom row, left to right:
Locker hooking, Chapter 7
Inlay with locker hooking, Chapter 8
High-speed knotted shag, Chapter 2

Back cover:
Bess chet on a cheater's warp, Chapter 21
Freeform fish rug, Chapter 8

Afterword

I suspect that there aren't many authors that ever feel that their book is "done," but there comes a point at which the final period gets placed. I know very well that this book isn't complete because at most it is only an overview of the delightful variety of rugs which can be made on frames. An entire book could be devoted to any *one* of the techniques covered here—and there probably will be.

It is my hope that all of you who have suffered from "loom-envy" are now mostly cured—and inspired to become rug makers. For my die-hard weaving friends, I also hope that you have been inspired to try out some frame techniques. For everyone, I hope that I've inspired your own textile explorations with this handbook and your curiosity about the field of rug making.

About the Author

Trained as a wildlife biologist, and with a long family tradition of textile skills, Mrs. Gray has demonstrated a unique talent for researching and being able to reproduce old rug making techniques. Beginning in the 1970s, she also experimented with new textile structures and in the 1980s began writing about rug making. When asked about her purpose in documenting the hundreds of rug making methods, she told the *Idaho Arts Journal* in 1987, "I am the door through which others will walk." Her goal has always been to teach others to make rugs and thereby preserve the methods for future generations. Mrs. Gray lives with her husband in the mountains of Idaho.

To Learn More about Rag Rugs and Rug Making, Visit the "Rugmaker's Homestead" on the Web.

This comprehensive website includes articles about all of the varieties of rag rugs, their history and construction. Current sources of supplies, tools and books about rug making are listed, along with links to resources, suppliers and traditional rug makers.

http://www.rugmakershomestead.com

Printed in the United Kingdom
by Lightning Source UK Ltd.
117557UKS00001B/229